Tales of the Unexpected

Tales of the Unexpected

The Power of Jesus' Parables

Melvin Tinker
with
Nathan Buttery.

CHRISTIAN FOCUS

Melvin Tinker is Vicar of St John's Newland in Hull. His other publications include *Alien Nation* (Christian Focus Publications, 2001, ISBN 1-85792-677-3) and *Road to Reality* (Christian Focus, 2004, ISBN 1-85792-958-6). Melvin is married to Heather and they have three boys.

Nathan Buttery's first degree was in Latin and Greek, then after a few years working as a Youth Worker in North London he did another degree, this time in theology and became the Assistant Minster at St. John's Newland in Hull. Nathan is married to Debbie.

Copyright © Melvin Tinker & Nathan Buttery 2006

ISBN 978-1-84550-116-0

10 9 8 7 6 5 4 3 2 1

Published in 2006
by
Christian Focus Publications,
Geanies House, Fearn, Ross-shire,
IV20 1TW, Scotland

www.christianfocus.com

Cover design by
Moose77.com

Printed and bound by
Nørhaven Paperback A/S

Contents

Preface

'Every picture tells us a story.' The genius of Jesus as a communicator was his ability to paint a picture with every story he told. Some of these 'parables' are simple similes— 'the kingdom of heaven *is. like* a man who sowed good seed...'. Others are simile stories, as with the labourers in the vineyard, while others are example stories, the best known being the story of 'The Good Samaritan'. These parables, often taken from everyday Palestinian life, aimed not simply to 'inform' people about the nature of God's rule, which Jesus came to establish (the kingdom of heaven), but to *transform* people's lives. In other words, they were part of the *means* Jesus used to secure that saving rule in men and women's hearts. Sometimes Jesus' parables had the effect of getting people to see things differently as he provided a new lens through which to view reality aright.

Other parables provoke and challenge people into action. They perform more than one function, helping us see things we have not seen before and at the same time making us reflect upon where we stand and what we are going to do with this new insight. By enabling the hearer to 'get inside' the story, perhaps by identifying with some of the characters or themes, Jesus disarms us. He gets in below our radar, which would otherwise cause us to erect defences to offset his teaching. Jesus speaking in parables may at times have left the crowds puzzled or affronted. They may have laughed or cried, but one thing is certain, they were never bored.

This book will suit Christians and non-Christians alike. It seeks to allow Jesus' parables to do their God-intended work. This involves providing some explanation of their original setting in the life of Jesus' ministry and relating them to our present day.

The book began life as a series of sermons delivered at St John's Newland. Jesus preached the parables, so we have tried to follow suit and where possible to keep something of the direct nature of the original sermons.

We would like to express our deepest gratitude to Joanna Tinker for her tireless work in editing the manuscript. Also our thanks go to the congregations of St John's and their encouragement in being good 'hearers and doers of the Word.' Lastly, we would like to express our appreciation of our wives, Heather and Debbie, for their unceasing support in our ministry.

Soli Deo Gloria.
Melvin Tinker and Nathan Buttery.
St John's Newland, Hull, 2006.

1

The Power of Parables

Matthew 13: 1–23

We had been praying for Tom and Sarah for a long time, so long we had almost given up hope. They were two ordinary students who were living lives that ordinary students are supposed to lead: eating, drinking, sleeping, and occasionally working. After a while, however, both of them became interested in Jesus Christ, and then, eventually, to our complete joy, both of them appeared to become Christians. It seemed to be a happy ending to a long story. At least, that was how it was for the first few weeks. Both came to church, both read the Bible, both met with Christian friends to talk about Jesus. But, after a few weeks, it became clear all was not well. Tom began to get some strange ideas about what being a Christian meant. He never came to terms with the change in lifestyle that following Christ entailed. He found church difficult and in the end he just gave up. Sarah, however, seemed to blossom. She did not find things easy, but she did stick at church. She went on a Christian camp in the summer, she found a decent church to go to when she moved cities, and she took Jesus seriously. As far as we know, she is still going strong as a Christian. Two students, one gospel, two responses. Why did that happen? Two people who appeared to start so well, but only one is still going ten years down the road. Why? That is the question we are left asking! Why do people respond in different ways?

If we had been with Jesus following him around, seeing the things that happened in the early chapters of Matthew's gospel, then we would be asking the same 'why?' question. Matthew has made it clear who Jesus is. He is the Saviour and King promised in the Old Testament, who is here to rescue people from their sins and to bring about God's kingly rule in their lives. There can be no better news than that. And yet already Jesus has faced opposition. It has been mounting in chapters 11–12, to such an extent that the religious establishment have decided to kill Jesus. So when we get to the end of chapter 12, we are beginning to ask several 'why?' questions about Jesus: 'Jesus, if you are the king as you say you are, why do many people reject you? Jesus, if you are such a powerful king, how come there is still evil in the world? Jesus, if you and your kingdom are so great, why does this kingdom of yours seem so small and insignificant? Jesus, if your followers keep getting flack for following you, why should they bother with you?' Those are the questions being asked; questions we ourselves may be tempted to ask. We look around and see our friends rejecting the gospel. We look at our nation and see the kingdom of God ignored and despised. We look at our lives as Christians and find hardship and struggle. So we ask the question, why? Why is it this way? And it's exactly those questions Jesus stops to answer in this chapter of Matthew.

Matthew places this chapter at the heart of his gospel, like an intermission that helps to explain some key truths about the kingdom of God. The way Jesus answers these 'why?' questions is by teaching seven parables or stories in which he teaches us important spiritual truths about the kingdom of God. One key phrase which crops up in this chapter is 'the kingdom of heaven is like such and such'. So, these parables teach us about the nature of that kingdom.

The first parable is the well-known parable of the sower, or, to be more accurate, the parable of the soils. This answers the question, 'Why do people respond in different ways to the message about Jesus?' It is clear the passage is about the word of God, or the gospel, because Jesus says as much in his interpretation of the parable: 'When anyone hears the message about the kingdom' (v. 19). Jesus teaches three things about the message of the kingdom of God and the Word that extends that kingdom: God's word is divisive (vv. 10–17); God's word is rejected (vv. 18–22); and God's word is fruitful (v. 23).

GOD'S WORD IS DIVISIVE

The first thing we learn about God's word, or the message of the kingdom, is that it is divisive (vv. 10–17). It may seem strange to begin in the middle of the passage, but once we have understood this part of it, we will be in a better position to understand this parable and the whole of chapter 13. Jesus has told the story to the crowd, but a little later, the disciples ask Jesus in verse 10: 'Why do you speak to the people in parables?' They ask him this question privately, and the interpretation of the parable is given only to the disciples, and that is key to understanding why Jesus speaks in parables. Jesus uses parables as a filter, or a sieve. To the casual observer these parables are just nice stories. Most of the crowd were in this category. They could not, and did not want to see the spiritual truth contained in this teaching of Jesus. But to those who wanted to know more, and who were keen to follow Jesus, the parables made them ask questions and made them think. The disciples show they are followers of Jesus by their desire to find out more. So there are two kinds of reactions: some want to think and know more about what Jesus has said others are turned off. God's word is divisive. It invariably divides people.

But Jesus also explains why there is this division in humanity, between those who reject his teaching, and those who accept it. There are two complementary answers. The first reason for this division is that God reveals the truth to people: 'The knowledge of the secrets of the kingdom of heaven has been given to you, but not to them' (v. 11). The disciples have had this truth about the kingdom of God revealed to them. God has opened their eyes. The truth is, we cannot make ourselves understand about Jesus. We are sinful to the core and natural rebels against God. The only way we can have our thinking turned around to worship God, instead of hating him, is for God to reveal the truth to us and open our blind eyes. And what a relief that is, because it means our salvation is in God's hands. God reveals his truth to people. And by definition, says Jesus, that means others do not have the truth revealed to them.

Before we think that is unfair, there is a flip side to this coin which Jesus explains in verse 15. He quotes from the prophet Isaiah. God told Isaiah the people would reject his message, and the reason for this rejection was entirely the responsibility of the people. Thus we learn our second reason for the division. People are responsible for their decision about Jesus. So Matthew quotes Isaiah as saying: 'This people's heart has become calloused [or, hardened]; they hardly hear with their ears, and they have closed their eyes' (13: 15). The people have deliberately closed their ears to the message of Jesus. They have walked away and so they will be judged for their rejection of the Saviour. That is what the second half of verse 15 means. It is not that Jesus does not want to rescue people; rather, people do not want him to rescue them. In one sense, they do hear the message in that they hear the parable, but in another sense they do not hear; they do not penetrate below the surface meaning, so they fail to understand.

Think of it like this: you are about to go on holiday. To get to your destination you have to take a plane. And when you go on a plane there are the usual safety announcements telling you where the exits are, how to put on your life jacket and so on. But how many people listen to the announcement? Almost no one. Yes, in one sense all the people hear. You cannot fail to since they turn up the sound so much. Yet in another sense they do not hear, because it goes in one ear and out the other. And when it comes to a crash, they will be found wanting, because they have ignored the safety briefing and will not know what to do. They will have to take responsibility for their fate because they heard the safety message and ignored it.

Jesus, then, is telling us two things. First, God chooses to reveal his truth to some and we cannot understand that truth without his revelation, and second, at the same time, we are responsible for whether we accept it or not. Those truths may seem contradictory, but throughout the Bible they run in parallel: God's sovereignty and our responsibility. Yes, God is sovereign, but we are also responsible for our actions. And so, to come back to the parables, the reason Jesus speaks in parables is to filter out his hearers. Those who follow Jesus and want to know more will seek the truth of what he is saying; those who have will be given more. But those who do not want to know will hear, yet not understand. And tragically, the more you hear, the more hardened your heart will become; even what you have will be taken from you. If you fail to respond to the light God has given you, then even that light will be taken from you. Your rejection of Jesus becomes your judgement.

God's word is divisive. The evangelist sees that every time the gospel is proclaimed, some reject the message, others accept it. Of course, some will accept it later, after having initially rejected it, yet still the division stands. Those who accept the message, whose hearts are softened to God, and those who reject Jesus, whose hearts are hard. And the parables show up that division as clear as day.

Following the success of the film 'Titanic', an exhibition was mounted. It was a fascinating exhibition of various bits of the Titanic that different rescue ships had picked up in the mid Atlantic. It was clear the ship was a marvellous place to be if you were wealthy. But there was one obvious thing in that exhibition: although there were three classes of passenger on that ship, depending on wealth, on that cold night in April 1912, there were only two classes of passenger. At Southampton Docks on the day following the disaster, there was a notice which had two lists, showing the two classes of people: those known to be saved, and those known to be dead. The great divide on that ship was no longer based on wealth, but on whether you were rescued or not.

Jesus teaches us in this passage that there are two types of people in the world: those who are saved and those who are lost. It depends on our response to Jesus. The question that immediately arises is: which category are you in? Have you accepted the Word, or rejected it? Either way, God's word is divisive.

GOD'S WORD IS REJECTED

Having looked at this central section first, let us move on to the parable itself, as we see Jesus' second point: God's Word is rejected (vv. 18–22). Jesus' parable works out some of the applications of how people respond to God's Word, or the message of the kingdom as Jesus says in verse 19. It explains what happens whenever the gospel is preached, whenever the farmer sows the seed, whether the farmer is Jesus or us today. The story itself is straightforward and would have immediately rung bells in the minds of his audience. Jesus uses a homely example to make his point: a man sows some seed—a common sight in ancient Palestine. The seed lands on four different types of ground: the hard-trodden path; the shallow, stony ground; the thorny ground; and the good, rich soil. The first three all die after a while: the first is eaten by birds straightaway, the second scorched by the sun, and the third choked by thorns. Only the last survives—it takes root and bears a huge harvest. That is the story. Later, however, when he is alone with the disciples, Jesus explains the parable. The common thread with the first three types of soil where the gospel seed lands is that the word is rejected. It may look as if there is genuine acceptance and growth, but sooner or later, the seed dies. The problem is not with the seed—the message of the gospel—but with the soil where it lands, that is, the person the gospel is given to. Notice, too, that in each of these three cases, Jesus says the person hears the message. The problem comes in what happens next.

The Path

Firstly there is the seed that lands on the path: 'When anyone hears the message about the kingdom and does not understand it, the evil one comes and snatches away what was sown in his heart. This is the seed sown along the path' (v. 19). This person hears the message about Jesus, and yet, instantly, the devil snatches the message away. Their heart is so hard there is no chance for the word to take root in their lives. It is the person who perhaps comes to a church service, but simply walks away with no thought whatsoever of accepting the message. The chilling thing Jesus tells us is the devil is at work to take away the seed. The Bible makes it clear that if we are without Christ then we are going the devil's way. So any attempt to share the gospel with others is, by nature, a spiritual battle.

The Rocky Ground

The next type of soil where the seed lands is the rocky soil: 'The one who received the seed that fell on rocky places is the man who hears the word and at once receives it with joy. But since he has no root, he lasts only a short time. When trouble or persecution comes because of the word, he quickly falls away' (v. 20). Notice that this person again hears the word, and even receives it with joy, and yet, down the track, they are shown up for their shallow profession. This person seems at first to be going well; they are full of joy, and involve themselves in everything. As time goes by, however, it becomes clear that they never put down any real roots. Their faith is so shallow that, when trouble strikes, they dry up and wither away; all fizz, no substance. They have no spiritual backbone to get them through the tough times of life. There is a serious danger that many Christians may be like this; enthusiastic at first, yet so busy doing church things there is no time to read the Bible and develop their relationship with God. So, when trouble strikes, either persecution for the faith or other suffering like unemployment, bereavement, financial stress, or illness, there is no anchor to hold them. Their faith is shown for what it is—rootless and hopeless. They are spiritual fireworks: loud and exciting for a few brief moments, and then nothing.

The Thorny Soil

Then there is the thorny soil: 'The one who received the seed that fell among the thorns is the man who hears the word, but the worries of this life and the deceitfulness of wealth choke it, making it unfruitful' (v. 21). This is the most challenging to twenty-first-century Christians. How many Christian lives are slowly choked to death by worry and materialism? You may not be able to detect it on any given day, but over the months and years, slowly this professing Christian is dying. Yes, they keep coming to church, but Jesus has little impact on their lives. All sorts of weeds grasp at the throat of this little shoot, slowly draining it of spiritual life, until at last it is just a lifeless twig. Wealth is perhaps the biggest killer. Not that money in itself is wrong, but the love of it has shipwrecked many a faith.

The true story is told of a rich London banker who died, and who had wanted the hymn 'Guide Me, O Thou Great Jehovah' at his funeral. The third verse was supposed to go: 'When I tread the verge of Jordan, bid my anxious fears subside; death of death, and hell's destruction, land me safe on Canaan's side.' But there was a misprint on the order of service, and, instead of saying, 'land me safe on Canaan's side,' it read, 'land my safe on Canaan's side.' The trouble was that it summed up his life: a professing Christian who loved money more than God. You do not have to be a rich banker to love money more than God. We always want that little bit more, and the way we spend our time and money reveals our priorities. Then there is worry, another weed to sap our spiritual life. Jesus said: 'Come to me, all you who are weary and burdened, and I will give you rest' (Matt. 11: 28). Do we believe that? If so, we are to do it, and not let the thorns get their hands on our spiritual throat.

We see three ways in which the seed is rejected, and yet it is not the seed that is the problem; it is the soil, the heart of the individual. The seed may be rejected immediately, or it may take longer, but, whichever it is, it is finally rejected.

GOD'S WORD IS FRUITFUL

Lastly, we see that God's word is fruitful—the fourth soil: 'But the one who received the seed that fell on good soil is the man who hears the word and understands it. He produces a crop, yielding a hundred, sixty or thirty times what was sown' (v. 23). Like all the others, this person hears the word, but, unlike all the rest, he or she understands it. The word takes root in their life and they produce a wonderful crop. The key is not so much the greatness of the crop, but that fruit is borne. Fruit in the Christian life is seen in all sorts of ways, but perhaps we could sum it up by saying that the person who truly accepts the gospel loves and obeys Jesus Christ. They long to pray, to grow in holiness, to be more like Jesus, to use their time, money, and energy for the kingdom of God, and to share their faith with others. That is the fruitful person, the one in whom God's word has taken root and is growing. Sometimes the progress will be slow, at other times more steady, but over the months and years, there will be growth. For where God's word takes root, it will bring back a wonderful harvest in the life of the believer.

Jesus asks each person a very important question: which soil are you? Are you the person who has rejected the gospel straight off? Then be aware of what you are doing. You are rejecting the only one who can save you. Or are you stony soil? Is your faith so shallow that when the tough times come, as they inevitably will, you will not have enough spiritual roots to survive? Or are you thorny ground? Are other concerns and the deceitfulness of wealth slowly draining your faith away? Or are you growing and bearing fruit for your Saviour? Unless we are growing, however slowly, we are in danger of being found out as one who started well but who in the end fell away. We are not to rest on our spiritual laurels or to think we have made it. We are to keep growing and bearing fruit.

So when we ask Jesus the question, 'Why do people respond in different ways?', he gives an answer. He tells us God's word is divisive. He tells us God's word is rejected. But he also tells us God's word is fruitful. Then he turns to ask us a question: What are you doing with the word of God?

2

While We Were Sleeping

Matthew 13: 13–24

Lavender Hill. What a wonderful name for a town. It sounds so idyllic. What image does it conjure up for you? A community of cosy, suburban tranquillity perhaps? It is, in fact, a run-down Black Township on the edge of Cape Town in South Africa. It is a scene of abject poverty, the like of which many in Britain could not even begin to imagine. It is also a place of the most unspeakable evil. Armed gangs frequently engage in gun battles in the open streets with folk getting killed in the cross fire. Unimaginable things are done to children in the form of sexual abuse. Yet, amidst all this moral decay and spiritual darkness there burns a little light—a Christian church. When you enter that church with a congregation of about seventy, the presence of God is so real you feel as if you can almost touch it. What is more, there is a love that shines from the faces of everyone present; a love which is genuine and unforced. In short, it is a living miracle. What is striking is that this miracle of goodness sits cheek by jowl with evil. A policeman was shot dead just around the corner from the church in broad daylight. A decapitated body was once found lying on the church steps. After a confirmation class, four young girls set off from that church only to be raped in full view of a watching crowd in the middle of the road. When the minister tried to intervene he was told to 'leave well alone' or he would be killed. That is Lavender Hill.

If you are a Christian living in that environment, what questions might be going through your mind? 'Why doesn't God do something? Why doesn't he just come down and get rid of all those wicked and not so wicked people and be done with it?' Like the psalmist, our patience begins to wear a bit thin and we cry out, 'How long, O Lord?'

Jesus knew such a question would never be too far from the minds of his followers as they try to wrestle with the problem of why there is so much evil when God is so good? He knew we veer towards one of two extremes: undue optimism on the one hand, believing things are bound to get better as we try to capture the world for the gospel; or resigned cynicism on the other, a feeling of 'why bother? Let's just form our holy huddle and batten down the hatches.' Therefore, Jesus tells a parable intended to instil a balanced realism within his followers. It is the parable of the wheat and the weeds.

In verses 24–30 Jesus tells a story of a rotten piece of petty espionage. A farmer is getting on with his normal practice of seed sowing. In goes the seed of the best variety of wheat, it is 'good seed' (v. 24). When all the hard work has been done, he simply has to wait for the harvest. That is when someone engages in a dirty-tricks campaign. Thugs are hired to sneak in at night to contaminate and ruin the crop with 'weed seed'. At first no one notices a thing; one seed looks much like any other. But as the seeds germinate and begin to grow the differences become clear. For what has been sown is darnel, a member of the grass family, which is the spitting image of wheat except that it is a weed which has within its grains a poisonous fungus. Panicking, the workers rush back to the owner and suggest that they set about ripping up the weeds to save the day. But the owner knows that, by this stage, the size of the crop and the intertwining of the roots meant that would destroy both. The solution would be worse than the problem. No, it would be far better to wait, letting the two coexist until harvest time when the final sorting will take place.

Even before turning to the interpretation which Jesus gives in verses 36–43, it does not take a rocket scientist to work out that he is talking about what happens between Christ's first and second comings. Verse 24 has already told us that this word-portrait is a picture of the kingdom, and in the previous parable Jesus explained that he is the sower. He brings about his kingly rule in the lives of people by proclaiming the gospel, the seed of God's word, which, when implanted in people's hearts, transforms them. But what happens between that initial establishing of his saving rule and the final consummation of that rule? The answer is that good and evil prosper together. Jesus the sower is at work, but so is Satan. The question is: how are the followers of Christ to respond?

THE EVER-CHANGING, NEVER-CHANGING WORLD

The first thing we are to grasp is that we live in an ever-changing, never-changing world. From one point of view the world never seems to change. Why is there still so much evil in the world? Christianity has been around for some two thousand years, yet we still have wars, corruption, starvation, and crime. No sooner do we remove one tyrant from the world than he is replaced by another. It is like cutting off the head of a Hydra: another simply takes its place. In this passage Jesus is saying that is exactly what we should expect. This world is, after all, a battleground. Verse 38 tells us the field in the allegory is 'the world'. It is God's world which rightly belongs to King Jesus, the Son of Man (v. 37). Within this world a rebellion and a revolution are going on simultaneously; a revolution designed to overturn the rebellion. The rebels are described as 'sons of the evil one'. That is, whether they know and believe it or not, to a greater or lesser degree, non-Christians are serving God's enemy the devil: 'The weeds are the sons of the evil one, and the enemy who sows them is the devil' (v. 39). These are the weeds. Those are Jesus words. How is that rebellion expressed? According to verse 41 they cause 'sin and do evil'. Literally, they 'cause people to stumble and they are lawless'. This does not necessarily mean they are monsters, because nice, respectable, well-intentioned, and even religious people can be lawless and cause others to trip up, acting like weeds carrying a poisonous fungus.

So what do we think God, who gave us the wonderful gift of sex to be used in the proper context of marriage, is going to make of an academic journal which is read by clergy and students, called *Theology and Sexuality*? This publishes articles which contain the most vile and graphic descriptions of gay sex. One such article is entitled, 'A Place for Porn in a Gay Spiritual Economy.' Another argues that we have to find room for what is called 'erotic Christianity'. These articles are degrading in their explicitness and blasphemous in what they espouse. When an academic validation of a gay lifestyle is given like this, with at least the tacit approval of church leaders, leading people into not only a miserable existence, but a medically dangerous and a spiritually disastrous one, are we not entitled to think that is precisely the kind of 'causing to stumble and abandoning of his laws' Jesus has in mind here?

The causing to stumble goes on. Think of the advertisers who peddle the lie that all meaning and value is to be found in what we eat, what we wear, and how we look. The result is that young girls are eating more and more, yet getting thinner and thinner and becoming more and more miserable. Or think of the big lie that there is no God and that the field in which we live is not cultivated at all. This is the humanistic view that there is no sower and no wheat, for we are all weeds, wild and free, so 'who cares—do your own thing'. Sincerity is not the issue, but who we serve is. Yes, from one point of view, the world carries on as much the same wicked world it always has been.

UP THE REVOLUTION

From another point of view, the world has been changing fast because the revolution is under way. The King has come to reclaim his world and has been busy forming a people to populate it; these people are called 'sons of the kingdom' (v. 38). He has enabled them to switch sides, freeing them up to become the people they are meant to be, whose destiny is to shine like the sun in the kingdom where God is their Father (v. 43). As that gospel spreads, and more and more people become part of this new worldwide revolutionary movement, the world changes for the better. After all, who stopped the terrible practice of widow burning in India? The answer—Christians. Who changed the labour laws in this country so little children were no longer sent up chimneys, sometimes working up to sixteen hours a day? Christians. Who brought about prison reforms so men, women and children were no longer thrown together into rat-infested holes, but were treated with dignity and care? Again, Christians. Every major improvement in the well-being of humanity can be traced back to the influence of Christians, not atheistic humanists.

A few years ago in that little Lavender Hill church, a group of American doctors came over to offer their services free to the community. Over a thousand people came through those church doors not only to receive medical aid but also to hear of the love of the Lord Jesus. That is our world: two groups of people serving two masters, and we belong to either one or the other.

BE PATIENT

The second lesson this parable teaches is a demand for patience without lapsing into indifference.

Behind the servants' question, 'Do you want us to pull out the weeds?' (v. 28), is the impulse to act now. This would be impractical, however, because the two plants are intertwined and they could not harm the weeds without also harming the wheat. That clear separation of the good from the bad can only take place at the end of time in the final judgement. When you think about it, you can see why. For a start, appearances can be deceptive. Just by looking at someone, can you tell who is a true believer and who is not? Of course not! Can you look into peoples' hearts to see what they believe? Obviously not; only God can do that. As the parable of the soils or sower shows, some people appear to be Christians at the beginning and later prove not to be, so we cannot have a premature judgement. Also, Christians themselves are not perfect and sin remains in them, therefore things are not as clear-cut at the moment as we may think. This is also why it is foolish and dangerous to be asking God to act in judgement upon others now, for unless we can claim total innocence it could well boomerang back on us. The author Dorothy L. Sayers puts this so well:

> 'Why doesn't God smite this dictator dead?' is a question a little remote from us. Why, Madame, did he not strike you dumb and imbecile before you uttered that baseless and unkind slander the day before yesterday? Or me, before I behaved with such a cruel lack of consideration to that well-meaning friend? And why sir, did he not cause your hand to rot off at the wrist before you signed your name to that dirty bit of financial trickery? You did not quite mean that? But why not? Your misdeeds and mine are nonetheless repellent because our opportunities for doing damage are less spectacular than those of other people. Do you suggest that your misdoings and mine are too trivial for God to bother about? That cuts both ways; for in that case, it would make precious difference to his creation if he wiped us both out tomorrow.

The fact that wheat and tares coexist in this world and are inter-linked with each other helps to explain why Christians, also, get caught up in tragedies. The Bible is clear that the world is under God's judgement and some of that judgement is being worked out in the present; that is the Apostle Paul's argument in Romans 1. The book of

Revelation is full of pictures of judgement being exercised in this world in terms of famine, war, and the like. In a wicked world that turns a deaf ear to God, when calamity strikes it is meant to get our attention, reminding us, all is not well between us and our Maker—we need to repent. After all, Christians and non-Christians died in those twin towers in New York on 9/11. In a similar incident in his own day when a tower collapsed, no doubt killing godly Jewish believers, Jesus said these people were no more sinful than anyone else, but they were sinful nonetheless, and turning to the crowd he said, 'Unless you repent, you too will all perish' (Luke 13: 3). We live in a messy world and God's judgement in the present is also messy as the results of sin work themselves out indiscriminately. The wheat is mixed with the weeds.

The problem is, when Christians look at the world and the awful things people do, they tend to react by going towards one of two extremes.

The first is to become impatient. That the church exists in the world means the world will, to some extent, be in the church; wheat and weeds exist within church fellowships. It is here that an impatient Christian says, 'I don't like this, I am going to form a pure church. I don't like this nasty world so I am going to withdraw from it.' But we know what happens. That church splits further and further in its quest for purity until all that is left is, 'Me and thee, and I am not sure about thee!'

The other extreme is that of sheer indifference. Here the Christian thinks, 'Oh well, there is always going to be evil in the world and heretics in the church.' Therefore, with a shrug of the shoulders they say, 'So what? Live and let live.' But that is to abdicate our responsibility. Remember, this wheat is growing in the field and bearing fruit. Christians are called sons of righteousness. They should be working to promote righteousness by opposing evil in the world, and promoting what is good and wholesome.

Within the church they should be seeking the discipline of those who teach lies and think immorality is acceptable.

What we are called to exercise is patience. Yes, God is sovereign. He is working his purposes out, the kingdom is growing and judgement day is coming, so we are to get on with the job of spreading the Good News. This is another reason why God has not yet brought the final judgement about—he is giving people time to repent (2 Pet. 3: 9). These are the days of grace and mercy but they will not last forever. God may be showing his patience with us but he is not indifferent to us. What we have done matters to him and we need to take him seriously because he takes you seriously, which means taking these warnings of Jesus about judgement seriously as well.

A CRY TO HEAVEN, ASKING FOR HELL

Judgement postponed does not mean judgement denied, which brings us to the final point: there is a cry to heaven asking for a hell. Look again at these solemn words of the Lord Jesus and take note:

> As the weeds are pulled up and burned in the fire, so it will be at the end of the age. The Son of Man will send his angels and they will weed out of his kingdom everything that causes stumbling and all who practice lawlessness. They will throw them into the fiery furnace, where there will be weeping and gnashing of teeth. Then the righteous will shine like the sun in the kingdom of their Father, he who has ears let him hear.

Ours is a self-contradictory society. On the one hand, a new commandment has been added to the Decalogue, forming the eleventh commandment: 'You shall not judge'—'Who are you to tell me what I can and cannot do, what is right and wrong? It is all relative so do not judge.' But on the other hand, when faced with wanton evil, suddenly no punishment can ever be enough. The Christian sociologist, Peter Berger, notes how in the debate over the architect of

Hitler's Jewish extermination programme, Adolf Eichman, there was a general feeling that 'hanging was not enough'. He points out that in the case of some human deeds no human punishment will ever be enough. He writes: 'It's our experience in which our sense of what is humanly permissible is so fundamentally outraged that the only adequate response to the offence as to the offender seems to be a curse of supernatural dimensions.' He goes on to say that, 'deeds that cry out to heaven also cry out for hell.' In other words, there are deeds which demand not only divine condemnation, but divine damnation. It was Winston Churchill who once said that the evidence that 'God existed was the existence of Lenin and Trotsky, for whom hell was needed'. These words of Jesus are not so wild and extreme as they may first appear. They simply reinforce what we all instinctively feel: that we cry to heaven for a hell so true justice can be satisfied; so justice is done and seen to be done.

This is where history is heading—judgement day—because our lives do count for something and they must be weighed and evaluated. The results are terrifying—'weeping and gnashing of teeth', a picture of terrible punishment. 'Ha', we may say, 'it is just picture language Jesus is using, it is figurative and is not meant to be taken literally'. Exactly! If that is how terrifying the picture is, how much worse do you think the reality is going to be? Jesus is not playing games here, he is being deadly earnest.

That is why it is vital that we get on-side with the rightful owner of the world now before it is too late. The clock is ticking and with every passing moment we are one step closer to eternity. That is why the good news is so wonderfully good. It saves us from what would otherwise be an inevitable fate, like the one the Lord Jesus describes here, and replaces it with a glorious destiny of shining like the sun in the Father's everlasting kingdom.

So which is it going to be? Joining the revolution, exercising patience in the face of evil, and working to transform it for the good? Or will it be adding further to the world's list of miseries by rejecting Jesus and so sealing your own fate? As Jesus said: 'He who has an ear let him hear.'

3

From Small Things

Matthew 13: 31–3

Here is a short extract from Mark Twain's, *Huckleberry Finn*, with part of a conversation Huckleberry Finn had with Mary Jane, the daughter of Peter Wilks who had just died. Huck has just told Mary Jane that her uncle, the Reverend Harvey Wilks, who was the vicar of a church in Sheffield, England, had no less than seventeen clergy on the staff, although, he added:

> 'Shucks, they don't ALL of 'em preach the same day—only ONE of 'em.'
> 'Well, then, what does the rest of 'em do?'
> 'Oh, nothing much. Loll around, pass the plate—and one thing or another. But mainly they don't do nothing.'
> 'Well, then, what are they FOR?'
> 'Why, they're for STYLE. Don't you know nothing?'

If 'style', by which we impress people, was important in the days of Huckleberry Finn, it has now been elevated to the status of a national obsession. Who we are takes second place to how we appear. The result is we are more concerned with the superficial than the substantial. Why else is the media consumed with celebrities—how they dress, what they eat, how they live? Sadly, the Christian church has not been immune from this either. Think for a moment about what was once considered the main purpose of the church—communicating the gospel. At one time, Christian speaking was seen as the art of conveying the understanding of truth. Increasingly, it has become a matter of performance and even pretence. Surveys show that only eight percent of an audience pays attention to the content of a speech, forty-two percent to the speakers appearance and fifty percent to how the person speaks. Style has triumphed over substance. Consequently, ours is the day of the 'telegenic' politician, the showman preacher—we like to be impressed with the impressive. In the words of another Twain, Shania Twain, we are often heard to say, 'That don't impress me much.' When the crowds started to gather around Jesus and began to hear his teaching about his kingdom, the new rule of God he had come to bring, they were not too impressed either. For them, the word 'kingdom' resonated with power and glamour, signifying the rule of Rome or Israel's heyday under King David. What were they to make of this northern itinerant preacher telling stories about seeds and farmers? Jesus was realistic enough to know that even his own followers would, from time to time, entertain doubts. Yes, there would be the doubt about God ruling when there is so much evil in the world, hence the parable of the wheat and the weeds. But then there are bound to be doubts about God's methods: 'how on earth can we even begin to believe that from some obscure teacher, surrounded by some obscure fisherman and quislings, in an obscure corner of the earth, God is going to change the world?' That is a mighty belief to swallow. Is not the temptation going to be to try to beat God, and, for the church, to ape the world by introducing some glamour and glitz? Invariably, it will be so. Knowing this, Jesus gives us two pictures designed to encourage us in the belief that God's ways are the best ways and the final results are going to be far greater than we could ever have imagined.

UNIMPRESSIVE BUT SIGNIFICANT

Firstly, we have the riddle of the seed, which makes the point that God's kingdom may be unimpressive but is definitely significant: 'The kingdom of heaven is like a mustard seed, which a man took and planted in his field. Though it is the smallest of all your seeds, yet when it grows, it is the largest of garden plants and becomes a tree, so that the birds of the air come and perch in its branches' (vv. 31–2). A contrast is made between what we start off with and what we end up with. What we begin with is far from impressive: the proverbial mustard seed. It is so tiny, about a millimetre in diameter. When the rabbis spoke about a minute drop of blood they spoke of a drop like a mustard seed. In other words, it is something you would hardly notice. If you were a visitor from Mars who knew nothing about seeds, you would take some persuading that from this tiny speck a bush would grow to about six to twelve feet high. Not only that, but the end result is so impressive that others benefit from it too; the birds come and shelter under its branches.

Do you ever look at a church congregation, while at the back of your mind being aware of the power of big business and the sweep of world politics, and think, 'This doesn't look much in the grand scheme of things. It is all pretty ordinary. What is the point of investing so much time, prayer, and energy into something like this? Is it going to change things?' Do you sometimes feel like that? It would be odd if you didn't. But that is the way it has always been, like looking at a mustard seed. Take the founder of this movement, Jesus. Born of a teenage peasant girl in a remote backwater of the Roman Empire and cradled in a manger, he lived in obscurity for thirty years in Nazareth, had a broad Galilean accent, with all the crude habits of that culture; he probably would have wiped his nose on his sleeve. Then, to die on a wooden cross and be buried in a borrowed tomb. Not impressive at all by any standards. His followers were not much better either. They were more of a rabble than an organised missionary group: fishermen; tax collectors; not a professional 'high–flyer' among them. There is the story of a bishop and his archdeacon discussing with someone what they would be looking for in a candidate for the ordained ministry. They stressed how important it was to be a good chap, have a good education, have the right background. So the man said, 'Would a medical doctor be ok?' 'Oh, yes', they said, 'Just the right kind'. 'What about a teacher?' 'Most certainly—you have to be able to communicate'. 'What about a coal miner?' 'Hardly!' 'A carpenter?' 'Oh, most certainly not'. And then the penny dropped as they realised, to their embarrassment, the faux pas they had made.

Our constant temptation as Christians is to play the world at its own game—to go for style in order to impress. If the world is taken with buildings, the church will build bigger and better ones, crystal cathedrals and all. If the world likes its hierarchies and titles, then the church will follow suit, with its reverends, venerables, and right reverends, with the garb to match. If the world is sold on entertainment, then there will be Christians who will want a piece of that action too; the glory of chart success or the movie contract. If it is what you look like that is going to make all the difference then Botox injections will be all the rage. It was interesting to watch an American Christian TV channel recently. An evangelist couple sat on gold thrones, surrounded by gold decor. The wife looked like a fifty-something Barbie doll who had obviously undergone surgery which was meant to impress. Of course it had to, because the content of the message left much to be desired. The result is we are left with a parody of the Christian faith—a mirroring of the world while wearing flimsy Christian dress.

The fundamental error behind all of these attempts to be 'with it' is trying to create heaven on earth, to have it all 'now'. The fact is, the seed is still growing, the bush is still spreading its branches and may not look much at all, but one day when Christ returns we shall be transfixed by the result. This is a kingdom that will embrace the whole world. What began in the tiny confines of Israel breaks out into the non-Jewish world, embracing people from every tribe and nation, rich and poor, educated and non-educated, all finding shelter and peace in the kingdom of the Lord Jesus. That is where the Church is heading. Already hundreds of millions around the world own the name of Christ— and it all began here in Matthew 13 some 2,000 years ago. Who would have thought it? But that is the power of this message. The wonderful thing is it is still doing the same today, changing lives by bringing people in touch with the true and living God.

HIDDEN BUT EFFECTIVE

The next parable, the riddle of the yeast, complements the first, for this kingdom may be hidden but it is effective: 'The kingdom of heaven is like yeast that a woman took and mixed into a large amount of flour until it worked its way all through the dough' (v. 33).

Here we are given insight into the method by which God's kingdom grows. The effect of the yeast is disproportionate to its size: a small amount of fermenting yeast mixed into about fifty pounds of dough to bake enough bread for 100 people—that is the picture. The yeast itself is hidden, mixed in with the flour and so penetrates and transforms the whole batch. This is the difference submitting to the loving rule of Jesus makes as we take his teaching seriously. It affects our lives as individuals, changing us from within. But it is also what happens when those Christian individuals and groups start to penetrate society. They may seem small and weak in comparison to the power brokers of the world, but the effects are startling and society as a whole benefits.

For example, Thalasius, a Christian monk founded the first institution for the blind. The first free dispensary was founded by Apollonius, a Christian merchant. The first hospital was founded by Fabiola, a Christian woman. Paganism does not produce compassion, Christianity does.

Paganism leaves sick, newborn babies on the hillside to die. Christianity takes them in to enable them to live.

Whatever sins and weaknesses beset the Church, we do have so much we can point to and say, 'Look at the effects of the kingdom.' Without doubt one of the greatest periods of social improvement was during the latter part of the eighteenth century and throughout the nineteenth century. Whereas France endured a bloody revolution in the name of Enlightenment, we enjoyed a spiritual revolution under the Evangelicals. But it did not remain in the heart alone, it translated itself into action to benefit other people. Even non-Christians recognised this. This is what Professor Halevey writes of the abolition of slavery: 'But to understand the delight with which the emancipation of the Negroes was greeted, the rejoicing which took place on a large scale throughout the entire country...we must remember that the abolitionist campaign had been first and foremost a Christian movement.' Or, thinking of improvements in popular education, one of the early editions of *Encyclopaedia Britannica* writes that this was 'a striking tribute to the sterling qualities of self help and religious earnestness which were so characteristic of the Early Victorian period.' Improvements in workers' rights and conditions can also be traced back to the influence of the Christian faith. Here is the late Jack Lawson MP, in his book *A Man's Life*: 'The first fighters and speakers for unions and improved conditions, were Methodist preachers. That is beyond argument. And the gospel expressed in social terms has been more of a driving power in northern mining circles than all the economic teaching put together.' It is this gospel which transformed our land.

Often the beginnings of what turns out to be a worldwide and lasting influence can be so small. Here is an example which began in Hull in 1770 and is still having its influence felt thousands of miles away on the other side of the world. Joseph Milner was the head teacher of Hull Grammar school, which then was next to Holy Trinity Church in the market place. He was a churchgoer, even ordained, but it was by reading Hooker's sermon on Justification that he became converted, realising he could not save himself by good works but needed saving by what Jesus had done for him on the cross. The result? Friends dropped him like a hot potato. Respectable people would walk on the other side of the street rather than talk to him, because he had become tainted with the 'E' word—he had become an Evangelical, a man who took the Bible seriously and lived it. He used to preach at Holy Trinity in the afternoons and people would crowd. Drunks and prostitutes became Christians and were changed. He started to train up and encourage men into the ordained ministry, many of them his former pupils. By 1790 it was said that almost every pulpit in Hull was occupied by an evangelical—that included St Mary's Lowgate which had an amazing young man called John King. Now the interesting thing is this: it was through the influence of Milner that Richard Johnston became the first chaplain to Botany Bay, Australia. He was then followed by Samuel Marsden, who then went on to be the first missionary to New Zealand. The present Diocese of Sydney, which is almost uniformly Evangelical, can trace their spiritual ancestry back through these men to Milner, and so to Hull.

Here we can see how, under God, the influence one man or a group of people can have. Milner had no idea what the twenty-first century church in Sydney would be like. All he was doing was attempting to be faithful to his Lord by using the gifts and influence God had given him to make a difference for good, and, like yeast, allowing the wholesome transforming power of the Gospel to do its work.

Surely that is what we need today? We need communities of yeast working quietly and effectively in our towns and cities. We are not to underestimate our influence as Christians in the workplace, in our street, or with our children, as prayerfully we simply witness to the Lord Jesus

Christ. We are to leave the results to God because a little yeast and a small seed can go a long, long way.

4

Caught and Taught

Matthew 13: 47–52

One Sunday afternoon in early June, Richard Van Pham set off in his twenty-six-foot boat, 'Sea Breeze', from the coast of California, in Western America, for Catalina Island. Unfortunately, he met with disaster and this short three-hour trip became a three-month odyssey. A storm came up, which broke his mast and outboard motor. Shortly after, his radio also failed. He could do nothing except wait for help. At the mercy of storms, winds, and tides, Mr Van Pham's food ran out after a week. He had to catch birds and grill them for food, while collecting rain water for drink. When he ran out of fuel for the grill, he began to chop up bits of the boat. His plight was further complicated by the fact that he has no living relatives, so no one reported him missing. He just had to sit tight. He never gave up hope, however, and a passing American frigate eventually rescued him off the coast of Guatemala, 2,500 miles from his original destination. Yet, even when the crew came alongside, Mr Van Pham tried to get them to fix his boat so he could sail home! He was finally persuaded that his boat was dangerously close to sinking, and gratefully accepted the rescue. 'I am very, very happy!' he was reported to have said. It is a true story of a man whose destiny was changed when he accepted the hand of rescue.

In the parable of the net we find Jesus teaching us about our destinies. He warns us about the possibility of being permanently separated from God forever when we die. In this, his last parable in this block of teaching, he points us to the future and gives us a warning. For, he says, there will be a great separation of humanity when we will be divided, and we will receive our destiny based on how we have responded to Jesus. After all his teaching, Jesus asks us a question: 'What will you do with Jesus?' Are you ready to face the future? Like the sailor we began with, we face a terrible future if we reject the rescue, but, if we accept it, our future is secure; our destiny can be changed.

REMEMBER THE SEPARATION

The first lesson to learn from this parable is to remember the separation; to remember that there will be a division of humanity at the end of time: 'Once again, the kingdom of heaven is like a net that was let down into the lake and caught all kinds of fish. When it was full, the fishermen pulled it up on the shore. They sat down and collected the good fish in baskets, but threw away the bad' (v. 47). So it is a simple story about fishing: some fishermen go fishing and, in the traditional fashion, they pull a net between two boats and trawl the lake for fish. They catch all sorts of fish, some good and some bad. The Old Testament gave instructions on what fish the people of God could and could not eat, so those they could not eat were thrown away. That is the story. So what is the point? Jesus tells us: 'This is how it will be at the end of the age. The angels will come and separate the wicked from the righteous, and throw them into the fiery furnace where there will be weeping and gnashing of teeth' (v. 49). This story is about the end of the age—the time when Jesus will return to wrap up history—so this parable is different from that about the weeds. There Jesus told us to be patient and to be encouraged because although there are weeds and wheat co-existing in the world at present, one day God will sift the crop. This parable, however, focuses simply on the end when there will be a great separation of mankind.

Firstly, Jesus tells us how this separation will take place: 'This is how it will be at the end of the age. The angels will come and separate the wicked from the righteous' (v. 49). So the separation will be between the wicked and the righteous. It is tempting here to think that Jesus is saying God will judge between good and bad people, and which of us would put ourselves into the bad category? 'We are all good people', we would probably say. 'We are not evil people: we love our children; we help our neighbours; we recycle our papers; we don't kick the cat! We're good people!' The problem is Jesus is not using our criteria to judge us. He is using God's, and, by God's criteria, we are all in the wicked camp, for in the Bible, to be wicked is to be someone who does not keep God's law perfectly. That is his standard. Each one of us has failed to keep God's law one hundred per cent of the time.

An advertisement recently appeared on the internet:

> You're in serious trouble—It's a proven fact. Deleting 'Internet Cache and History' will not protect you, because any of the web pages, pictures, movies, videos, sounds, emails and chat logs and everything else you do [on your computer] can easily be recovered and come back to haunt you. How would you feel if a snoop made this information public to your spouse, mother and father, neighbours, children, boss or the media? It could easily ruin your life.

We are then encouraged to buy this company's product, which will presumably prevent such information being found on our computers. The people who wrote that advertisement know how human beings work. We all have things we are ashamed of others seeing or finding out about, and, in this modern age, some of them are on our computers. Or, if the world of computers is alien to you, imagine someone recorded every thought, action and word you said for a whole week and then played the video to your family. How would you feel? The sad fact is we do not even keep to our own standards, let alone God's. God's verdict on us is that we are by nature wicked, as Jesus says here.

The Bible tells us we are all wicked, and God will judge. All the wrongs of the world will be given their due justice. The problem with our world is that often justice cannot be done. Think about the people who got away with huge crimes in the last century. Hitler was never punished for his crimes as he committed suicide before he could be caught and tried. Timothy MacVae was killed for the Oklahoma bombings and yet he took over 200 lives. The September 11 bombers were never brought to justice because they died. Has justice been done? Have they paid properly for their crimes? The Bible tells us that one day they will; they will have to stand before God's court and receive their punishment. What is more, God will be perfectly fair. Of course, the only problem with a perfectly fair justice system like God's is that we are all guilty. We must all stand before him.

If we are all wicked, who are the righteous? There must be some or the angels will not have any separating to do. Well, of course, the great news is that there is a means by which we can move from being wicked to being righteous in God's sight. There is a way for our guilt to be taken away, and that is if our sins are taken by another. That way is Jesus himself. He died on the cross to ensure that we need not stand before God's judgement seat guilty, but instead, we can be forgiven, cleaned up, and made right with God, which is what righteous means. Amazing news! It is not an offer we deserve; God extends it to us out of his mercy and love through Jesus. So, when the angels come to separate the people at the end of time, they are not separating good people from bad people as we might understand it; they are separating people who have ignored or rejected Jesus from those who have accepted him and his offer of rescue. That is the only difference between the wicked and the righteous: either we trust Jesus to take our sins or we reject him.

This truth should come as a wonderful relief to all of us. According to Jesus, no longer do we have to impress God with our good deeds, or try to con him into thinking we are good enough. We are not, and the sooner we realise it the better. The only way we can be right with God is to trust what Jesus has done for us on the cross. Whether you have been a Christian for years or days that is a wonderfully comforting truth to remember. We are sinners saved by grace, not works. This is what divides mankind. Those who have accepted Jesus and those who continue to trust in their own efforts to get to heaven.

In America, there is a large rock in the Rocky Mountains called the Dividing Rock. As water crashes down on this rock, the water is divided into two different rivers. They end up in different destinations. One river goes to the Pacific Ocean, the other to the Atlantic. On the rock of Jesus, humanity is divided and separated. Our decisions for or against him have massive implications, for not only must we remember the separation, but we must also recognise our destiny.

RECOGNISE YOUR DESTINY

Jesus does not simply tell us there will be a separation at the end of time; he also tells us what that separation will lead to: the wicked will be thrown 'into the fiery furnace, where there will be weeping and gnashing of teeth' (v. 50). He reminds us about the destiny of the wicked—those who reject the rescue of Jesus Christ on the cross—and that destiny is hell. The concept of hell is sometimes difficult for people to grasp. Hell is often parodied as a place where the horned devil with a pitch fork tortures people. It is a place where, a friend of mine once said, 'you meet up with all your old friends and have a wicked time'. But hell is no joke. In fact, the one person that speaks most about it in the

New Testament is Jesus himself—gentle Jesus, meek and mild. He is the one who tells us about hell. This phrase, 'the weeping and gnashing of teeth', comes up seven times in the gospels and is only ever used by Jesus. Whilst the language may be in some sense pictorial, the pictures Jesus paints are meant to convey the awful truth of a place of unimaginable horror.

The reason hell is such an awful place is because it is where God's wrath against sin is seen in all its fullness. Too often we think of God as a gentle old grandfather who would never say 'boo' to a goose. He is the sort of person who says to us with a wink: 'Have you been doing naughty things again?' and then slips us a sweetie and gives us a cuddle. But that is not the God of the Bible. God shows himself in the Bible to be a God of perfect holiness, a God who cannot stand sin, whose wrath burns at the human pride and arrogance that puts us at the centre of our lives. In his justice he is rightly angry at anything which smacks of sin. That is why there is a hell; because anything which is sinful cannot stand in God's presence. So, to be in hell is to be separated from God forever, no longer enjoying the good things he gives us on earth like friendship and beauty. Hell is not a fun place to be; it is a place of almost unbelievable horror, which even the biblical pictures can barely explain to us. It is a place for those who say 'no' to God's loving offer of rescue. It is for those who willingly reject him, and continue to do so. God confirms them in their folly. He gives them what they want: life without him. That is hell.

So why does Jesus tell us about hell? He tells us because as a loving God he wants to warn us. And we ignore the warnings at our peril. There is a part of Canada where black bears freely roam. On all the paths and roads there are huge signs warning of the dangers of the bears. Whenever you go into a National Park you receive a leaflet explaining the risks. They make scary reading, encouraging you to watch out for bears and advising what to do if you encounter one. You are virtually surrounded by intimidating pictures of big, black bears with large, sharp claws and very nasty looking teeth. There are two possible reactions to such warnings: people could either say: 'Oh, they are trying to scare me. Bears are cuddly and cute. Why are they using these scare-tactics? They just worry the children more. I'll happily go through the forest and ignore the advice,' or they could say: 'The authorities don't want me to come to harm. That is a loving and caring thing to do. I'll heed the advice and take care.'

To a far greater extent, Jesus has given us a loving warning showing us where we are heading if we continue to reject the rescue he offers. If we ignore Jesus and say: 'Oh it can't be that bad. It's all scare-tactics,' then we are in danger of finding ourselves before a holy and just God with no saviour and no hope. Hell is no joke. It is not scare-tactics. The kindest, gentlest, and wisest man who walked the earth says that it is true. He gives us a way out.

But what of the destiny of the righteous, those who accept the rescue? Jesus has already told us in an earlier parable: 'Then the righteous will shine like the sun in the kingdom of their Father' (v. 43). We will be with God, forgiven and made perfect forever. There is no comparison, is there? So if you have not done so before, recognise where you are heading if you are not trusting Christ. Heed the warning and accept his rescue.

RESPOND TO THE CHALLENGE

Lastly, Jesus tells us to respond to the challenge in verses 51–2. He asks his disciples a question: 'Have you understood all these things?' (v. 51). He is probably referring to everything he has said since verse 36 as, from that point on, Jesus is alone in a house with his disciples. Have they understood all that Jesus has explained about the parables of the kingdom of God? Yes, they reply. They may not have got it all, as the gospels show us, but at least they have understood the main points. And so, as a result of their understanding, Jesus issues them with a challenge: 'Therefore every teacher of the law who has been instructed about the kingdom of heaven is like the owner of a house who brings out of his storeroom new treasures as well as old' (v. 52). So what is the thrust of Jesus' challenge to his disciples? His point is this: If you have it, share it. If you have understood, then the onus is on you to give it out. Literally, Jesus says to his disciples: 'Every teacher who has been discipled, or taught, in the kingdom of God'. These disciples have been taught the things of the kingdom and so they have treasure to give out. They have the treasure of the Old Testament which Jesus has fulfilled in the New Testament. Accordingly, they have old and new treasures to share. At the end of the gospel in Matthew 28: 19, Jesus gives his disciples a command which they are to keep obeying until the end, until Jesus comes again, which was to 'make disciples of all nations'. In verse 20 they are told to teach everything that Jesus has taught them. The teaching the disciples have received from Jesus is to be passed onto others. They are to be messengers of the kingdom.

When you think about it, verses 51–2 of chapter 13 make perfect sense in this context. If, as we have just heard from Jesus' story about the net, there is a division in mankind, and if everyone faces eternity either in heaven or hell, what is the disciple's natural response going to be? It will surely be to tell others. What news could possibly be more important than that Jesus is the one who can change our destinies? What news could possibly be more important than the news that we are facing hell unless we turn to Jesus to save us? There is nothing as important as that. Just as it is the most loving action of Jesus to warn us of the danger we are in, so it is the most loving thing we can to do to warn our friends and families of the peril they are in, to show them the Saviour and to urge them gently and graciously to come to Christ. That is the pressing challenge Jesus gives us: to be men and women who do all we can to show people the treasure of the gospel. Our love for Jesus and others compels us to share this treasure with others.

Telling others is not an option. It is a need. Having said to Jesus: 'I understand', he sends us out to do his work. Yes, it will be hard. Some will not want to hear. Yes, we will be afraid, because it is daunting showing people where they stand with God. Yes, it is painful, because our nearest and dearest face a future without God. But what did Jesus say to his disciples in Matthew 28? 'And surely I am with you to the very end of the age' (28: 20).

One man who took this challenge seriously was a man called John Harper. He was on the Titanic when it went down in April 1912, with the loss of 1,522 lives. He was a young pastor from Glasgow who was on his way to Chicago to lead a mission in a church. The Titanic was the most luxurious ship ever built to that day, and yet John Harper was not fazed by the extravagance of the wealth he saw around him. Instead, he gave himself as fully as ever to the service of his Saviour. The night before the ship went down, he was seen pleading with a young man on deck to trust in Jesus as his Saviour. His true zeal for God was seen in the final hours of his life: as everyone else was desperately trying to save themselves, John Harper was handing out life jackets and helping others onto life rafts. In his final minutes, as he struggled in the icy waters of the Atlantic, what was he doing? Pitying his life as it ebbed away? Cursing God for allowing him to get into this state? No, he was urging all around him to put their trust in Jesus. Four years after the Titanic went down, a young Scotsman got up at a meeting of Titanic survivors in Hamilton, Canada, and said, 'I am a survivor of the Titanic. When I was drifting alone on some wreckage that awful night, the tide brought John Harper near me. 'Man,' he said, 'are you saved?' 'No,' I said. 'I am not.' He replied, 'Believe on the Lord Jesus Christ and you will be saved.' The waves bore him away; but, strange to say, brought him back a little later, and he said, 'Are you saved now?' 'No,' I said, 'I cannot honestly say that I am.' He said again, 'Believe on the Lord Jesus Christ, and you will be saved,' and shortly after he went down; and there, alone in the night, and with two miles of water under me, I believed. I am John Harper's last convert.'

John Harper spent his life and even his final minutes urging people to trust in Jesus. He knew that people's destinies and eternal futures were at stake. He had taken up Jesus' challenge to share his treasure with others, and he did so passionately to his dying day.

Jesus makes it clear in Matthew 13 that one day he will return and judge the world; there will be a division in mankind. Each one of us faces either heaven or hell depending on our response to the Saviour. Nothing can be sweeter than John Harper's final words. 'Believe on the Lord Jesus Christ and you will be saved.'

5

Love from Unexpected Places

Luke 10: 25–37

A television producer once said, 'Our rule of thumb in showing human suffering is that the death of a thousand people in the Third World is equivalent to a hundred people in the West, ten adults in our own country, and one child in our local community.' In other words, human worth is relative. Those who are furthest from us, either in distance or type, are to be given less care than those closest to us. Of course this is nothing new. Aristotle argued that we should limit the reach of pity to 'people like us'. We often say, 'Charity begins at home.' The trouble is, it tends to stay there!

On the other hand, television has shown us the needs of a bigger world and we are now in danger of going to the other extreme. We can have such an idealised view of helping 'humanity' that it becomes easier to write a cheque for the hungry in Africa than to help the old man next door. One is reminded of the Peanuts cartoon with Lucy wearing a T-shirt which has written on it: 'I love humanity—it is people I can't stand!' But, it is people we have to deal with.

For those who profess to worship the one true God, this question of loving people and not just humanity involves high stakes; according to Jesus this is a test of whether we are on the road to eternal life. The real measure is not whether we can make creedal assent, that is saying what we believe, but whether we engage in Christian action, thus expressing Christian behaviour. This is spelt out for us in one of the most well-known, and yet often misunderstood, stories that Jesus ever told—the parable of the caring Samaritan.

A PROPER ASPIRATION

Luke's account begins with a man who has a proper aspiration: 'On one occasion an expert in the law stood up to test Jesus. "Teacher," he asked, "what must I do to inherit eternal life?"' (v. 25). Here is someone concerned about his eternal destiny. He recognises that what matters is not simply the 'here and now', but the 'there and then'— eternity. The question he asks, however, is not a genuine one. He raises it not to gain spiritual insight, but to score a theological debating point; Luke tells us he wanted to 'test Jesus'. He thinks he knows the answer and Jesus does not. After all, he is an 'expert in the law', that is, someone who has been to the finest theological college and qualified as a full-time professional Bible teacher. So the real intention in asking this question is to embarrass Jesus, with a desire to see this self-appointed preacher fall flat on his face.

A PERTINENT ANSWER

In a wonderful turning of the tables, what Jesus does is to get the man to answer his own question. It is obvious he wants to show off his Bible knowledge, so Jesus gives him an opportunity to do just that, and in so doing gives him enough rope by which to hang himself: '"What is written in the law?" he replied. "How do you read it?"' (v. 26). At this point the man decides to impress Jesus by quoting two remote verses from the Old Testament, one from Deuteronomy and another tucked away in Leviticus, providing a pertinent answer: 'He answered: "Love the

Lord your God with all your heart and with all your soul and with all your strength and with all your mind;" and, "Love your neighbour as yourself"' (vv. 27–8).

When you think about it, the man is right. Here is the perfect summary of the whole Old Testament law which is all to do with right relationships: being rightly related to God and to one another. This is the essence of covenant. In these two texts we have the embodiment of the Ten Commandments, the first four of which all have to do with living before our Maker so that he is number one in our lives, and the last six are about the way we live with one another. Love God; love your neighbour. 'Do this', says Jesus, 'and you will live.'

But that raises a big question: how do you know whether you have done it? How do you measure whether you are loving God with your whole being? Is it simply by how much time you spend thinking about him, how intensely you pray to him, or how often you sing to him? If our eternal destiny is dependent on what we do, as this man obviously thinks—'What must I do to inherit eternal life?'—then it is crucial that we have some standard by which we can measure our success. You need a benchmark to which you can point to comfort yourself that you are on the right track. And maybe that is why the man opted to keep the second commandment as the mark of spiritual progress, skipping over the first commandment, when he asks 'Who is my neighbour?' At least there you can see evidence of true piety, for you either treat people badly or well. If it is the latter then you must be OK, if it is the former, then you are not. That is how many people see it. In fact, the first commandment about loving God has disappeared from view altogether, leaving only one commandment in the twenty-first century: 'Love each other.' And, 'Who needs to be a Christian to do that? Anyone can qualify. So, even if there is a God, then this is all he will look for in me when I roll up to the pearly gates when I die.' We often think like the late Tony Hancock in the classic 'Blood Donor' sketch that we will be able to take out our blood donor card, as well as a list of all the charities we have contributed to, and tell God to 'tot that up', expecting him to be impressed. Maybe you think that. You feel you are 'not all that bad'. You have never done anyone any harm and you look on yourself as a 'decent sort of person'. Perhaps you can go further: you are 'religious', with an impeccable pedigree, having been brought up in a Christian home, having regularly read your Bible notes, even attending a sound church and able to quote the Bible with ease, just like this man, so you must be 'well on the way'. But the question forces itself to the surface again: how do you know you have been good enough? That you have done the right things to the right people? What we tend to do is to fix things so that we can be sure.

A TWISTED ATTITUDE

How can a rail company make sure trains run on time? They change the timetable so the formerly late time becomes the new, correct time. How can an examination board improve the pass levels? Simple: make the exams easier. The name of the game is accommodation. The religious leaders of Jesus' day were brilliant at doing just that. For them the way of ensuring the keeping of the law was by making it easier to keep—they employed the principle of minimum requirement. That was behind the question of the Bible expert in verse 29 which revealed a twisted attitude: 'But he wanted to justify himself, so he asked Jesus, "And who is my neighbour?"' From beginning to end his view of salvation was all about justifying himself. He thought he had to do something to inherit eternal life; he wanted to justify himself, not only to Jesus or to himself, but ultimately to God, so he throws out the question with a knowing smirk: 'Who is my neighbour?' If the number of people we are to be kind to in order to get to heaven is small enough that would be manageable, at least in theory. The religious elite of Jesus' day had an answer to this question: their neighbour was a fellow Israelite. The text from Leviticus 19: 18 taken literally seems to imply this, for the first part reads: 'Do not seek revenge or bear a grudge against one of your own people, but love your neighbour as yourself.' So are we back to Aristotle, showing love only to one of our own kind? No, because Jesus in this parable does two things which blow such narrow-mindedness out of the water. Firstly, he shows there are times when we do not manage even to do that. Our self-interest is such that we do not help one of our own, so we fail miserably and we will not get into heaven that way. But secondly, he asserts the principle of maximum application versus minimum requirement. He does this by relating a shocking account.

A SHOCKING ACCOUNT

The first part of the story could have been taken straight from Palestine's News at Ten. Such brutal incidents were all too common. The road from Jerusalem to Jericho was a well-travelled and notoriously dangerous one. It was literally a case of 'going down' that road, for Jerusalem was 2,700 feet above sea-level and Jericho 820 feet below. This meant a drop of 3,500 feet over a seventeen mile journey through desolate and craggy limestone hills. It was ideal bandit country. That is why many of the people travelled in groups. It was a scary and risky business. Jesus' listeners would not have been surprised to hear his description of a man beaten, stripped naked, robbed, and left bleeding to death on the open road—it happened.

It looks, however, like all is not lost; help is on its way. It may not be the arrival of the cavalry, but it is the priesthood: 'A priest happened to be going down the same road, and when he saw the man, he passed by on the other side' (v. 31). A profound disappointment! But it is possible to shrug your shoulders and say, 'There is always one bad apple in the barrel isn't there? But look, here comes a Levite'. And so hope raises its head once more. The Levite, however, does the same. Here are the two pillars of the religious establishment—a priest and a Levite. Let us ponder this fact for a moment. The priests were the clergy responsible for offering the sacrifices in the temple at Jerusalem. They lived and breathed Old Testament religion, including Deuteronomy and Leviticus. They not only heard the Old Testament scriptures daily, they taught them. The Levite's job was to help them, especially in providing music and ensuring temple security—these were the worship leaders and bouncers of the temple. And what do they do here? Nothing! Imagine a paramedic seeing a cycle accident and driving on—that is the picture we have here. It should not happen!

At this point some commentators begin to make excuses for them. Some say, 'they may have thought the man was dead, in which case they would not have been able to do anything anyway,' or 'it would have been dangerous to stop because they could have been mugged.' The word used in verse 30 translated 'half dead' could mean he was in such a bad way he appeared dead and so was beyond help. Or it could be taken that he was so badly beaten he was on the verge of death and therefore needed help. Given that the next person who came along did take action seems to indicate it was the latter, so there is no excuse. But secondly, some draw attention to the fact that for these religious people to 'touch' a dead body would have made them ritually unclean, and, since they were no doubt going on to do temple business, that was a risk they could not afford to take. But this will not do either, because Jesus says the priest was going 'down' the road—the implication being that it was in the same direction as the man, that is from Jerusalem to Jericho. That makes sense because Jericho was the place for the rich and famous to live—that is where the 'Posh and Becks' of the day would have had a villa. It had a wonderful climate and was known as the 'City of a Thousand Palms'. So these people were not hurrying to get to work and serve God, they were hurrying to get home and have a holiday, which makes their callousness all the more deplorable. Whatever reasons they had for not helping the man—fear of personal danger, thinking they were too late, ritual uncleanness— simply demonstrate that for all their talk and religion, some people are not willing to show love even to one of their own. Therefore, even when we do draw the circle closely, we fail. It is not as if the priest and Levite had hurt the man, they simply did not help him, and in God's sight that is just as bad. There are sins of omission, as well as sins of commission. Have you ever seen someone needing help, but because of an appointment or fear of embarrassment you have moved on, looking the other way, hoping someone else will do something? If so, then you have been the priest and the Levite.

Yet, everyone knows how hypocritical the clergy can be! But what about an honest-to-goodness fellow Jew putting the clergy to shame? That would make a good story. And perhaps that is what the listeners were expecting Jesus to say next. But he did not. The person he chose to be the hero could not have been more repulsive and offensive—in fact, it was plain sickening. He chose a Samaritan (v. 33). You can tell how seething the hatred was between the Jews and Samaritans by the fact that in verse 37, when Jesus asked who was the real neighbour in the story, our theological whiz-kid could not even bring himself to say the word 'Samaritan', he just managed to mutter, 'the one who had mercy on him'. The name stuck in his throat. There was no such thing as a good Samaritan, by definition. The Jews looked on Samaritans as religious and ethnic half-breeds. The animosity which existed between them went way back to Old Testament times. When the Samaritans built a rival temple on Mount Gerazim in 128 BC the Jews took a force and burned it down together with most of the city; not exactly the best way to win friends and influence people! The Samaritans were just as bad: a couple of years before Jesus was born a group of them broke into the Temple of Jerusalem and, on the Passover, scattered human bones around the place, thus defiling it. They were religious vandals. And so, when Jesus introduced the Samaritan into the story, you can be sure the people expected the Samaritan to simply finish the job.

But this one did not. On the contrary, he did the unthinkable—he helped the man. Make no mistake, his action was risky and costly. It was risky in that he too made himself vulnerable to attack, for he got down from his donkey and, later when he placed the man on the donkey, he extended the risk of attack even further as he would now be slowed down. He took wine and oil, antiseptic and balm, to soothe the man's wounds. All of this is so ironic, because the priest and Levite would have carried both of these things in their backpacks to be used in religious festivals, and yet here this semi-pagan Samaritan is putting them to proper use. But it was also costly: he paid for the man to be taken care of, and we notice how in verse 35 he is willing to reimburse any extra cost. That is love.

But why did he do this? Because 'when he saw him, he had pity on him' (v. 33). That is the difference. In fact, that is too weak a translation. The word used is that for 'moved with compassion', literally, 'his guts were churned up.' The only other times that word is used in the Gospels is to describe Jesus when he saw people in need—his stomach was churned up.

Now do you understand what was happening? When the Samaritan came by, what did he 'see'? He did not see a Jew. He did not see an enemy. He saw someone in need and was moved! What is more, he was moved to do something. So Jesus implicitly answers the question: 'Who is my neighbour?' Anyone in need is my neighbour. There are no religious, racial, or social limitations. In effect, he is saying to the scribe, 'Don't dare ask the question, "Who is my neighbour?" so that you can cop out in helping someone while simultaneously satisfying your smug self-righteousness!'

Jesus, however, pushes it one step further, for in verse 36 he says, 'Which of these do you think was a neighbour

to the man who fell into the hands of the robbers?' The
lawyer wanted to know the limits of neighbourly love so
that he could get away with the bare minimum, hence the
question, who is my neighbour? Jesus turns it around and
asks what sort of neighbour he should be. The answer: one
who shows mercy without limit.

Why, then, should we be like the religious no-hoper
Samaritan? The answer: because God is like this. The
Samaritan's response was Jesus' response—he was moved
with compassion. That is the pitiful irony here. The ones
who were supposed to represent God, who knew their
Bibles backwards, who were steeped up to their necks in
religion and ceremony, that is the priest, the Levite, and
the expert in the law, were least like him; whilst the one
who was supposed to be only a little higher than vermin
on the Israelite scale of values was most like him, for he
had 'mercy'. Is it not sad that sometimes the most religious
people can be some of the most hard-hearted people?

Yet, there is even more to it than that. When God looks
at us, he too sees a people battered and on the verge of
death; helpless and hopeless, unable to heal themselves
of the spiritual sickness called sin. He too is moved with
compassion. He climbs down from the glory of heaven,
making himself vulnerable in taking to himself human
flesh, and opening himself up to the same bad-mouthing
abuse normally reserved for Samaritans. In one incident
in John 8: 48, the religious leaders were so antagonistic
towards Jesus they accused him of being a Samaritan and
demon-possessed to boot; the worst insult they could fling
at him. Had they called him a dog, it would not have been
as bad. But he took the insult and, like this man, he binds
up our spiritual wounds by being wounded on our behalf;
as the prophet Isaiah says: 'By his wounds we are healed'
(Isa. 53: 5). That is why he made that journey towards
Jerusalem, along the same road, as he came from Galilee
and made his way to a cross. All of this underscores the fact
that we can do nothing to inherit eternal life, but he has

done everything. And those who have received his love are meant to show that same love to others as a sign of salvation, not as a means of salvation.

That is where the double challenge comes to us.

Firstly, are you still trying to do something to put yourself right with God? If so, forget it. You cannot. Swallow your pride and accept his mercy. Stop trying to justify yourself.

But supposing you are a Christian, then what are you doing to show it? Jesus' words to this man are his words to us: 'Go and do likewise.'

6

Temptation from an Unexpected Source

Luke 12: 13–21

Men who trap animals in Africa for zoos in America say one of the hardest animals to catch is the ring-tailed monkey. For the Zulus of that continent, however, it is simple. They have been catching this agile little animal with ease for years. The Zulus base their method on knowledge of the animal. Their trap is nothing more than a melon growing on a vine. The seeds of this melon are a favourite of the monkey. Knowing this, the Zulus simply cut a hole in the melon, just large enough for the monkey to insert his little paw to reach the seeds inside. The monkey will stick his paw in, grab as many seeds as he can, then start to withdraw it. But he cannot get his paw, clutching so many seeds, out of the hole. His fist is now larger than the hole. The monkey will pull and tug, screech and fight the melon for hours. But he cannot get free of the trap unless he gives up the seeds, which he refuses to do. Meanwhile, the Zulus sneak up and grab him. The monkey's greed catches him out in the end.

In this passage we find that Jesus' main theme is greed: 'Watch out! Be on your guard against all kinds of greed; a man's life does not consist in the abundance of his possessions' (v. 15). Jesus is in the middle of a teaching session with his disciples, when a man, who wants to settle a difficult dispute with his brother, interrupts. It involves money, but Jesus will not be drawn. Instead, he uses this question as an opportunity to teach his disciples about the dangers of greed. This section of teaching is part of a chapter where Jesus' concern is that his disciples be counter-cultural in their actions and attitudes. To understand the passage correctly, we need to understand the context.

At this point in Jesus' ministry, there were two problems. Firstly, there was opposition from the religious leaders, evident in Luke 11: 53–4: 'When Jesus left there, the Pharisees [that is, the religious leaders] and the teachers of the law began to oppose him fiercely and to besiege him with questions, waiting to catch him in something he might say'. Jesus and his disciples were beginning to come under pressure, partly because Jesus had just berated the Pharisees for their hypocrisy. But, whatever the reason, it cannot have been easy to bear. You can imagine one or two of the disciples may have been tempted to give up at this stage. A second problem was popular acclaim for Jesus from the crowd: 'Meanwhile, when a crowd of many thousands had gathered, so that they were trampling on one another, Jesus began to speak first to his disciples' (12: 1). Thousands were following Jesus. This time the temptation for the disciples was to lap up the crowd's favour, to enjoy and pander to them, perhaps to sign the odd autograph, and to be taken in by popularity and acclaim. At the heart of both problems, persecution and popular acclaim, there is the same temptation—fear of man; wanting to be a man-pleaser, wanting the love and support of the crowd. In the face of persecution, fear of man would drive them to quit. In the face of popular acclaim, fear of man would drive them to pander to the crowds and play to the gallery. So at this point Jesus addresses his disciples and warns them not to fall into the trap which was also the Pharisees' trap, because the Pharisees were men-pleasers. They were sham religious hypocrites who just played to the crowd: 'Be on your guard against the yeast of the Pharisees which is hypocrisy…' (12: 1). Do not be a man-pleaser, he is saying. Instead, 'Fear him who, after the killing of the body, has the power to throw you into hell' (v. 5). Fear God, not men. Do not seek man's approval; seek God's. That is how a disciple of Jesus should act. He puts it in a slightly different way in verse 31: 'Seek [God's] kingdom, and these things will be given to you as well'. Disciples of Jesus should fear God and seek first his kingdom. They should be counter-cultural.

In this context, it becomes easier to see why Jesus answers the questioner in verse 13 as he does. Jesus spots in this man a weakness to which his disciples must not succumb—greed. The disciples of Jesus are to be rich not to themselves, but to God. So, he says in verse 15: 'Watch out! Be on your guard against all kinds of greed; a man's life does not consist in the abundance of his possessions.' Greed is to be alien to the Christian because he or she fears God and seeks first his kingdom. As Jesus says in verse 21, we are to be rich towards God first and foremost. And while Jesus' primary application is to possessions, greed affects many areas of life. Are we truly rich towards God as Jesus will challenge us? Are we counter-cultural in this area of our lives, or have we fallen prey to this temptation of greed? The alarming truth is that if we fall short in this area, God's verdict on us on judgement day will be 'you fool' (v. 30). That is not a verdict anyone wishes to hear. This parable and its surrounding context highlights three temptations that Jesus warns us against, which are all driven by greed.

'GET-CENTRED' RATHER THAN 'GIVE-CENTRED'

The first temptation Jesus tackles is the temptation to be 'get-centred' rather than 'give-centred', that is, greed affects our attitude to others (v. 13):

> Someone in the crowd said to him, 'Teacher, tell my brother to divide the inheritance with me.'

> Jesus replied, 'Man, who appointed me a judge or an
> arbiter between you?' Then he said to them, 'Watch out!
> Be on your guard against all kinds of greed; a man's life
> does not consist in the abundance of his possessions.'

At first sight we might think there is nothing wrong with
this man who asks the question. It was the norm for people
to ask rabbis like Jesus for help in settling family disputes.
But Jesus is no ordinary rabbi. He will not involve himself
in a domestic squabble. There is something far more
important to be worried about which this man has not
understood: Jesus sees something in this man which leads
him to take him to task and to warn him publicly. For a start,
the man butts into Jesus' teaching session without a care in
the world. He is out of sync with what Jesus has just been
saying. Jesus has been impressing upon his hearers the need
to fear God rather than men. But this oaf butts in and says:
'Sort out my domestic, Jesus!' That is the tone. He does not
say: 'Jesus, can you possibly give us a little help on this one
please'. He says: 'Tell my brother to divide the inheritance'
(v. 13). But Jesus sees inside the heart to show that the man's
real problem was not the injustice of being wronged but
the evil of greed. 'Watch out! Be on your guard against all
kinds of greed' (v. 15), he says. Why? Because: 'a man's life
does not consist in the abundance of his possessions' (v. 15).
Wealth is not necessarily the problem. It is the abundance of
it; having far more than we need. A greedy person always
wants more and more, far beyond what they need, and
when you are greedy for more you will do anything to get
it. That was the problem for this man. He will do anything,
it seems, to get hold of his share of the cash, even to the
extent of climbing over his brother to do so. Greed ruins
relationships. It seriously affects our attitude to others. The
more you have, the more you want.

That was the case for one wealthy woman. She was
a billionaire who owned a string of hotels, and, at one
time, the Empire State Building. Yet, in September 1989,
Leona Mindy Rosenthal Helmsley was convicted of

thirty-three counts of tax evasion, for which she faced the possibility of 100 years in prison. According to *Time Magazine,* she emerged as a penny-pinching tyrant who tried to get money out of just about everybody. No amount of money was too small to fight over. After the sudden death of her only son at age forty in 1982, she sued and won most of his estate, $149,000, leaving his four children with $432 each and his widow with $2,171.

What does Jesus say to us? Watch out! Beware of all types of greed. Greed simply uses and abuses people to get what we want. The problem is it is so easy to fall into that trap. Even in the smallest ways we use and abuse people, often those we profess to love, to get what we want and to have it our way. Even Christians are prone to squabble over the inheritance from a relative, metaphorically, biting, kicking, and punching their way to get it. Jesus says that is wrong.

It is not just material greed he is talking about here. He says to us, 'Watch out for all types of greed': greed for power, perhaps a promotion at work to the detriment of others and our Christian witness; greed for a member of the opposite sex. Paul uses this word several times in his writings and he often uses it in the context of sex. Is that your weakness? Sexual greed? Maybe using your boyfriend or girlfriend to satisfy your own lustful appetites to their cost? Greed, perhaps, for someone you want but cannot have? Greed is so destructive. It destroys relationships. No wonder Jesus warns us against it! And it is at this point that he warns his disciples to be counter-cultural, because when Christians go against the grain of popular culture in their contentment with 'their lot', it makes an impact on the watching world.

SELF-CENTRED RATHER THAN 'GOD-CENTRED'

Jesus highlights a second temptation and that is to be self-centred rather than 'God-centred', that is, greed affects our relationship with God. He tells a parable to explain his main point, which is that a man's life does not consist in the abundance of his possessions. This man has a much deeper spiritual problem. Greed is affecting his attitude to God. He was far more interested in himself than God (vv. 16–19):

> And Jesus told them this parable: 'The ground of a certain rich man produced a crop. He thought, "What shall I do? I have no place to store my crops." Then he said: "This is what I'll do. I will tear down my barns and build bigger ones, and there I will store all my grain and my goods. And I'll say to myself, 'You have plenty of good things laid up for many years. Take life easy; eat, drink and be merry.'"

Let's see what this man would look like in the twenty-first century. He would probably have had a modest education and always worked hard. He had done his O Levels or GCSEs and then his degree. From his first job as a junior clerk in a big company, he gradually worked his way up the corporate ladder. Oh, it had taken time, and it had taken its toll: more than one broken relationship on the way. But now, at the age of fifty-three, he was on top of the world. He had a lovely house in the country with two acres and a gleaming new Jaguar in the drive. From time to time he sailed off the South coast in his small yacht. The children loved their schools—Elizabeth was getting used to her new horse; David was mastering expensive and dangerous new sports. His wife loved the Country Club. Everything was going well, even his wise new investments in Chelsea Football Club. He would soon be investing in more shares. To cap it all, he has decided to retire early. 'Oh, you're so wise,' they said at the retirement party. 'Get out of the rat race, put your feet up. Live off the fat of the land.' Now the guests have gone, the party is over, and as he lies back in the pool, the sun setting behind the imported Japanese pagoda, the man sips champagne and thinks to himself: 'You are very lucky. You have everything you have ever dreamed of. You've made it. Now all you need to do is take life easy, eat, drink and…'. Suddenly there is a searing pain in his chest. Before the ambulance could get to the house, he is dead.

To us, this man looks like the complete self-made man. He is a success in every sense of the word. Yes, he has had a few blips on the way, but, by and large, he is a success. But what does God say? 'You fool' (v. 20). He is not wise at all. He is a fool. Why? It is not because he is wealthy. The Bible is not against wealth. It is not even because he saved up and put some things aside. The Bible encourages us to be prudent and wise with our possessions and money. Neither is it because he has taken early retirement. Nothing wrong with that necessarily. The reason he is a fool is because he has not given God a second look. His world revolved around himself. He thought his life consisted in the abundance of his wealth. His motto was: 'The man with the most toys wins.' Notice how self-centred this man was. Did you mark how many times the word 'I', 'me' or 'mine' comes in the passage? Ten times, and he spends all his time talking to himself! He is even looking forward to the time when he will be able to talk to himself in verse 19. His world revolved around him.

We do not know what he was like. He may have been a nice person. He could even have been a religious person who believed in God. But his life told a different story. He was self-centred rather than God-centred. He failed to see that even his wealth was God-given. Notice what Jesus says: 'The ground of a certain rich man produced a good crop' (v. 16). It is as if Jesus is subtly reminding us that, for all our hard work, we are totally dependent on God's grace to make things grow. We deserve none of the credit. God alone gives us wealth, food, and clothing. Yet this man failed to see it. God's verdict? 'You fool!' And so Jesus concludes in verse 21: 'This is how it will be with anyone who stores up things for himself but is not rich towards God.'

Jesus' point is simple. He warns us that there is far more to life than getting as much as you can. Life has a different, more important purpose, and that is to be rich towards God.

People were made and designed for relationship with God, to enjoy and delight in him forever. If we are not doing that then we have missed the most important part of life, indeed we have missed the entire point. We might be successful, doing well in our job or studies, a model son or daughter, the sort of person everyone likes, with all the world's credentials attached to our name, but to have no room for God is to be a total fool. That is the divine verdict. It is not that God has not done amazing things for us. He has gone to extraordinary lengths to bring us back into relationship with himself. We are natural rebels against God, facing an eternity without him. But God in his love sent his Son to die for us so we could be right with him again. He became poor so we could be truly rich, not having more toys than anyone else, but able to be rich towards God.

The cross is God's way of declaring us rich in his eyes, forgiven and set free. If we ignore that gift and say, 'Oh it doesn't matter,' or 'Oh, I'll get there my own way,' then God will say to us: 'Fool! Why didn't you accept my offer?' There is no other way. We cannot get to heaven on our own merits because we are not good enough, nor will we ever be. A man's life does not consist in the abundance of his possessions. It is about something far more important.

We must remember the context here. Who is Jesus speaking to? His disciples. He warns them to be counter-cultural. In this area of putting self before God, those who profess to be Christians need to hear the challenge too. We cannot get off Jesus' hook on this one, because more often than not, we are rich towards self rather than God. Even if we have accepted God's gift of forgiveness and a fresh start, the temptation to put self first and God second is so strong. Greed has a nasty habit of getting in the way of our relationship with God. What does it mean to be rich towards God? Jesus' primary application in this chapter is to our wealth. He will go on to explain in the rest of the chapter that it means not worrying about our material wealth and trusting him. It also means using our wealth for God's kingdom and his purposes.

The problem for Christians in the affluent West is that the world screams at us: 'Do what you want with your life, get the GSCEs, get the A Levels, get the degree, get the job and get the mortgage'—none of which are bad in themselves. And so the first question we often ask is, 'What shall I do with my life', and not, 'What does God want me to do with the life that he has graciously given me?' The default is self, rather than God. But the God-centred Christian will ask: 'How can I use my gifts and time and energy and life for God's kingdom?' Our lives are not our lives at all. They are God's lives given to us for his glory and service. Maybe this will mean giving yourself full-time to God's work. The default for many Christians is to not think about it, rather than to think about it. God's harvest field needs more workers, and each one of us has unique gifts and talents to offer. Perhaps it will mean taking a job in a city where you know a church is being planted. It might mean a less well-paid job and a more basic lifestyle, but it will mean your time and energy can be devoted to that important gospel initiative. Perhaps it will mean reassessing our giving so we can give more sacrificially to support workers who are giving their time to share the good news of Christ. Admittedly, it is not glamorous and there may be great costs involved. We might have to re-evaluate our lifestyle, our families might not like it, and our non-Christian friends will think us mad. But that is what it means to be rich towards God. It means putting God and his kingdom first. 'Seek [God's] kingdom, and these things will be given to you' (Luke 12: 31). We need to be thinking gospel first and foremost, not 'self'.

The default setting on our thinking and priorities should be the kingdom of God, but the overwhelming tide of our culture tells us to think 'self' first, and we swallow it 'hook line and sinker' ninety-nine per cent of the time. Think God's agenda first. That should be the default setting in our hearts and minds, asking 'What is best for the gospel's sake?'

Not our personal comfort and plans. It will be different for each of us, but at least let's get into the pattern of thinking and acting that way, for too much is at stake. Jesus demands authentic discipleship.

'NOW-CENTRED' RATHER THAN 'FUTURE-CENTRED'

The last temptation is to be 'now-centred' rather than 'future-centred', that is, greed affects our relationship with time. This man in the parable was a fool not only because he forgot about his relationship with God, but also because he thought he had all the time in the world. He thought he would live to enjoy his hard-earned cash. The reality, however, was different: 'But God said to him, "You fool! This very night your life will be demanded from you. Then who will get what you have prepared for yourself?"' (v. 20). He was planning the rest of his life away, when in reality he had only a few hours to live. That is why Jesus is so urgent in this parable. He knows the reality and fragility of life. We are like flowers in the field, here today, gone tomorrow. But too many of us, non-Christians and Christians alike, live as if we were in charge of our destinies, as if we know exactly what will happen. We are too 'now-centred' rather than 'future-centred'. We forget that the most important event in our lives will not be the exams, the career, or even getting married; it is the great final exam before God— judgement day. That is the one event we need to be ready for. If we have invested all our time in this present world without a thought for the next, then according to Jesus we are total fools.

One of the excuses people often use to postpone thinking about Christianity is, 'I've got all the time in the world.' Jesus says: 'No, you don't.' We do not even know what will happen later this evening, let alone in thirty years, and none of us have a clue when our time is up. Think of those poor people in the Twin Towers tragedy in New York. That September 11th began like any other ordinary day, but for many it was to be their last. Some were ready for that day in that they were Christians. Many others were not. Ann Graham Lotz, the daughter of Billy Graham, talked about her feelings in the aftermath of the Twin Towers tragedy in this way:

> I was watching television the first day and saw interviewed a construction worker who had been an eyewitness through all of this in a building next to the World Trade Centre. He said, 'I've seen planes hit this building, people falling out of the sky'. He said, 'my heart is in my throat'. I feel like I would say the same thing. You almost don't have thoughts to articulate. Your heart is in your throat. You can hardly stand it. You're numb. For myself, I fall back on my faith in God and the foundation, speaking of those buildings, as an illustration of America, our foundation is our faith in God and the structure we build on that foundation is what enables us to endure something like this.... I believe God also knows what it is like to lose a loved one, as he gave his only son on a cross. He knows what it is like to see a loved one die a horrific death. He's emotionally involved in our pain and he has the answers to us and he can bring comfort beyond human understanding. Well, I pray that God will use this event to change us forever in a positive way. And that will strengthen our faith in him. I thought of all those people who have died in this tragedy. It doesn't matter right now what political affiliation they had or what denomination they belong to or what religion or what the colour of their skin was or their stock portfolio. What matters is their relationship with God. I would like to see Americans begin to focus on some of the primary things and some of the things that are more important than just, you know, entertainment and pleasure and making more money.

That is a poignant comment made in the light of Jesus' teaching here.

The question we are left contemplating is this: Will we be rich towards ourselves or God? Will we live for the present or for the future? The joy of the world to come should be a spur to us to serve God joyfully and faithfully knowing that every minute counts for God when you invest in heaven.

7

Lost and Found

Luke 15

A little boy sat on the floor with a piece of paper. He was drawing a picture with tremendous concentration. 'What are you doing?' asked his Mum. 'I'm drawing a picture of God,' came the reply. His Mum, not quite knowing how to respond, said, 'But no-one knows what God looks like.' He glanced up at her with an indignant look on his face and said, 'Well, they will after I've finished!'

Of all the pictures of God which people have conceived down the years few have been as evocative as that by Francis Thompson. In his poem, 'The Hound of Heaven', God is likened to a hunting hound relentlessly pursuing his prey, the author, not out of anger but out of love. This was true of Thompson's own experience. Having left his middle-class home in Preston to study medicine, he rebelled against his religious upbringing until, living diseased and destitute on the streets of London, he turned to the Saviour and was restored. Others, too, in their own experience testify to this dogged, almost ruthless, determined searching out by God. In his autobiography, *Surprised by Joy*, C. S. Lewis writes about his own conversion in these terms:

You must picture me alone in that room in Magdalene night after night, feeling, whenever my mind lifted even for a second from my work, the steady, unrelenting approach of Him whom I so earnestly desired not to meet. That which I greatly feared had at last come upon me. In the summer term of 1929 I gave in and admitted that God was God, and knelt and prayed: perhaps, that night, the most dejected and reluctant convert in all England.

This is a God who will simply not let go.

But who does God search out and favour? The religious leaders in Jesus' day had a ready-made answer to that question: he favours good religious people like themselves. If you wanted to be 'in' with God, the reasoning went, you had to be 'in' with their particular group. To put yourself outside the inner circle, which was defined by the keeping of the law and religious traditions, meant that you put yourself out of the reach of God's mercy. Therefore, the company you kept determined whether you were 'in' or 'out'. That is why they could not fathom Jesus. He broke all the rules and defied all convention for, in their own begrudging words, he 'welcomes sinners and eats with them' (15: 2). In this culture, to eat with a certain social group was a sign of acceptance, with 'sinners' being the religious outcasts who, because their lifestyle, could not join in with the normal Jewish ceremonies. Today if you want to join a political party you pay your membership dues and go along to the meeting, but at the time of Jesus if you wanted to join a religious party you went to a meal. Here Jesus seems to be joining the irreligious party. That was shocking. In the Pharisees' minds, for him to mix with these types would be equivalent to a surgeon shaking hands with a refuse collector before undertaking an operation and not washing—he becomes contaminated. Therefore, they thought it best to avoid them altogether. It all centres on distance. The religious saw the social dregs as distant from God and themselves as close to God. The way to keep close to God was by keeping away from those who were not. Tragically, there are people who act as if that is the case today. Some churches are so inward-looking you would not think there is a world out there which needs saving. But Jesus tells three stories which turn such assumptions on their head so that he brings close those who are distant, and shows to be distant those who think they are close. If we are going to feel the heartbeat of God and know him as he is, as well as experience the joy he feels, then we too must make sure that our thinking and actions are in line with his.

THE PRIORITY OF GOD'S LOVE: THE PARABLE OF THE LOST SHEEP

> Jesus told them this parable: 'Suppose one of you has a hundred sheep and loses one of them. Does he not leave the ninety-nine in the open country and go after the lost sheep until he finds it? And when he finds it, he joyfully puts it on his shoulders and goes home. Then he calls his friends and neighbours together and says, "Rejoice with me; I have found my lost sheep." I tell you that in the same way there will be more rejoicing in heaven over one sinner who repents than over ninety-nine righteous persons who do not need to repent.' (vv. 3-7)

'Look', Jesus is saying, 'no one would dream of criticising a shepherd for searching out one of his sheep if it had wandered off into the desert and been lost. It is part of what it means to be a shepherd, to leave those who are safe (probably with an assistant) and then to go out and look for that one sheep. That will be his priority. When he has found it, of course he will put it on his shoulders and bring it back and throw a party with his friends because he will be so overjoyed. That is what God is like.' Here in the person of Jesus is the Shepherd-King par excellence and in his ministry people are meant to see God at work. His priority is his heavenly Father's priority. His love is a searching love, not an insular love. When someone is brought back home, when a sinner repents (v. 7), it is an occasion for rejoicing not complaining. We may think of it like this: searching out the lost is not an option for God, it is an inner compulsion. This priority of God's love is even hinted at right back in the book of Genesis. After Adam and Eve rebelled and hid themselves in their shame and self-disgust, what do we read in Genesis 3: 9? 'The Lord God called to the man, "Where are you?"' Already he was seeking out the lost. He has been doing the same ever since.

THE INTENSITY OF GOD'S LOVE:
THE PARABLE OF THE LOST COIN

> Or suppose a woman has ten silver coins and loses one. Does she not light a lamp, sweep the house and search carefully until she finds it? And when she finds it, she calls her friends and neighbours together and says, 'Rejoice with me; I have found my lost coin'. In the same way, I tell you, there is rejoicing in the presence of the angels of God over one sinner who repents. (vv. 8-10)

Here a woman has lost a small silver coin, one out of a set of ten. She does not shrug her shoulders and say, 'Who cares? I still have the other nine'. Not at all! She pulls out all the stops to hunt down that single coin. Finding a tiny coin in a dark, peasant's house, open to the dust blown in off the streets, would be no easy task. If we want a modern-day equivalent, then think of the trouble someone has when they lose a contact lens. Every square inch has to be painstakingly covered and you cannot risk getting out the vacuum cleaner. The woman in the story lights a lamp and carries it around with her as she makes a careful sweep of the house. It is not surprising, therefore, that when she eventually finds it, with sweat pouring down her face, hot and flustered from all the energy she has just expended, she calls all the other women in from the neighbourhood. Out come the best crockery and the biscuits, and whatever the first century Jewish equivalent to a brew-up is takes place. In the original, verse 9 is more or less a command: 'You must rejoice with me.' It is all perfectly natural. This is what women do when they lose something valuable and then find it. So it is with God. He will go to whatever lengths are necessary to search out what was lost, he will not settle. When it is found, then naturally he celebrates: 'In the same way, I tell you, there is rejoicing in the presence of the angels of God over one sinner who repents' (v. 10).

A lost sheep, you will seek it. A lost coin, you will search for it. But what about a lost son? Of course, the stakes are higher. We are not talking about an animal. Nor are we dealing with a trinket. We are speaking about a son. Is there any instance when someone might not bother with their son? Surprising though it may seem there are circumstances when even a son might be written off in some people's minds, particularly if what he has done is bad enough. The family breakdown may be so severe and the relationship so distraught that the son or daughter might as well be dead. Sadly, it does happen. The people gathered around Jesus also knew there were times when a son (or a daughter) was 'beyond the pale' and not worth the effort. Jesus hands to them a prime example on a plate. In this story Jesus is saying: 'Think of a relationship so ruined, a son so repulsive that you would not want to know him, and I will show you a father who will stop at next to nothing to be reconciled to him.'

THE UNIVERSALITY OF GOD'S LOVE:
THE PARABLE OF THE LOST SONS

This is perhaps the best-known, and yet not necessarily the best understood, of Jesus' parables.

To grasp the stomach-churning action of the younger son you have to appreciate the nature of living in a 'shame' culture like this one. Unfortunately, our modern Western society finds it difficult to blush about anything, but for many who live in China, Japan, Africa, or the Middle East today, to bring dishonour upon one's family is almost unbearable to live with. To get a feel of the boy's action in the story and how the hearers would have responded, think of how you would respond if you saw a man in his twenties verbally abusing and demeaning a gentle old man in the street. You would be embarrassed, to say the least. But then, as this verbal tirade goes on, with all the shouting and swearing, you discover the person publicly humiliating the old gentleman is the man's son. Now you feel angry, you think, 'Who wants a son like that?' The poor fellow would be better off without him. That is what the crowd would have been thinking as Jesus told this story. By asking for his share of his inheritance now (v. 12), which amounted to about a third of the value of the property, the younger son was in effect saying to his father, 'Dad, I wish you were dead', for a son would not normally receive an inheritance until after his father had died. That is how much he rated this relationship. He wanted to shelve all his responsibilities, and his religion, by going away to what we can only assume is a Gentile country, a far country. By describing it in this way, Jesus conveys the severity of the separation—he could not have been further away from his father than this, as symbolised by the distance involved. In this culture, you did not treat your parents like that. 'Honour your father and mother' says the commandment. But this selfish, sorry excuse of a son does the exact opposite: he dishonours his father, and the crowd knew most fathers would not want to be associated with such a son. Indeed, it would have been less painful for such a family if the son had simply died in an accident. There would be no shame in that. Then, to add insult to injury, the blessings that God had poured upon this family over generations are squandered (v. 13—remember how important the promise of the land was to the people of Israel), until his money and his friends run out. When this Jew is not only reduced to feeding pigs, but willing to fill his empty, aching stomach with the pig swill, it looks like he is simply getting what he deserves—a fate worse than death.

Jesus gives us an insight into what the real problem is with the human race, and what it is he came to remedy.

If a sheep wanders off, it is simply doing what a sheep does, like bleating. If a coin gets lost, you equally cannot blame the coin. But when a human being is lost, he or she is responsible, as the son in this story is responsible for his situation. What we see enacted here between the son and the father is what every human being since Adam has been doing. We each in our own way have been thumbing our noses at God and saying, 'God, I wish you were dead'. Like the son, we do not always put it in such crude terms, but that is what our actions amount to. Like the son, we want to cast off any responsibility we have to our Maker. We wish to take his blessings and squander them on ourselves. We want God effectively to be absent from our lives. The result is that, like the son, we invariably go from bad to worse in trying to satisfy our empty soul with the pig swill of promiscuity, banal entertainment and vain spiritualities. Thus we ache, as individuals and as a nation. Some years ago, the journalist Bernard Levin wrote these words:

> Countries like ours are full of people who have all the material comforts they desire, together with such non-material blessings as a happy family, and yet lead lives of quiet, and at times, noisy, desperation, understanding nothing but the fact that there is a hole inside them and that however much food and drink they pour into it, however many motor cars and television sets they stuff it with, however many well-balanced children and loyal friends they parade around the edges of it…it aches.

We reach a key transition point in the story in verse 17 when we read that the son 'came to his senses'. He realises how stupid he was being; how even living as a hired servant back home would be far better than the so-called 'life' he now had. Carefully he rehearses a speech admitting his fault and asking his father to take him back on such terms, and then he makes the long journey home: 'So he got up and went to his father' (v. 20). We are not given any clear indication that the son was genuinely repentant, that he meant what he was going to say, but we can be certain that Jesus' hearers would have doubted its sincerity. You can imagine them thinking to themselves, 'Nice little speech that, but of course it won't fool anybody. Does he think his father is a complete imbecile? Just wait until he does get back, he will have to work off his debt and learn his lesson.' But whether it was genuine or not, the focus of the story (as with the other two parables) is not on that which is lost, but on the one who does the looking. The outcome of the story does not turn on the character of the son but the character of the father. Likewise, our salvation turns not upon what we are like, but upon what God is like. What is that?

Here is shock number one. The father behaves in a way which is out of keeping with the customs of the day. He sees the son coming at a distance: 'But while he was still a long way off, his father saw him and was filled with compassion for him; he ran to his son, threw his arms around him and kissed him' (v. 20). Far from washing his hands of him, he has been waiting for him day after day in longing expectation. He runs to meet him, something no self-respecting man ever did, as it was considered to be thoroughly undignified, but he does it nonetheless. Notice too that he does not even wait for the boy to finish the speech; unconditional forgiveness is immediately offered— he embraces his son and kisses him. Shoes are placed on his feet, these only being worn by freemen, thus showing that he was to be no slave. A ring is placed on his finger, a sign of authority over the household. The best robe, that is the robe of honour, is placed around his shoulders and the party to end all parties is arranged with the killing of the fatted calf, which would happen only on a few occasions in any one lifetime. The father is beside himself with joy! If you want a glimpse into the heart of God, you could not do any better than this.

Some people still picture God as the reluctant forgiver. Oh yes, he might have us back, but only after we have paid our dues and squirmed. Not so! He longs to have us back and to have us back immediately. Maybe you feel you have done things which cause you so much shame you could not even tell your best friend. It could be that, in your mind, God would not even give you the time of day. If so, then look at this story again, because that young son is you.

The father lays down no preconditions. It is a relationship he wants with us and he is big enough and generous enough to offer it. The question is: are we desperate and humble enough to take it?

Earlier we referred to this as the parable of the lost sons, plural, for there is another son in the story who was just as lost as the other, but did not realise it. Here is shock number two—it is the elder son. Note how he describes his relationship with his father. Why, it is hardly a relationship at all! He too acts shamefully. He does not even address him as 'father' in verse 29, something at least the younger son did. Instead, he views his father as a slave-driver: 'All these years I've been slaving for you' (v. 29). His father might as well be dead, as a father. This is a cold, impersonal business relationship he has set up. He has no family, at least in his own mind. In verse 30 he speaks of 'this son of yours'—not 'my brother'. He stays outside the family home when the party is in full swing. For all the warmth and intimacy of the relationship between himself and his father—he might as well have been on the other side of the world. Although he stands on the same property he could just as well have been in a far country. He too is lost.

In the other two parables of Jesus we see someone doing the searching—the shepherd and the woman. On first sight, it appears this parable is out of line with the other two, as the father never went out to look for the lost younger son. Perhaps that is because the younger son was not that far away from his father, at least in his own heart. He recognised his need and went to the only one who could meet that need. He was close to him in thought. But a closer look at this story shows that the father does go out looking for the lost son, the lost older son, and pleads with him to come in and join the rest of the family: 'The older brother became angry and refused to go in. So his father went out and pleaded with him' (v. 28). In verse 31 he reminds him that he is his son: 'My son', he calls him, 'your brother', he tells him, 'was dead and is now alive. We had to celebrate'. Of course! It is only natural.

This is the real lost son in the story—lost in his own self-righteousness and pride. This is someone who, in his own eyes at least, had never put a foot wrong: 'I have never disobeyed your orders' (v. 29). Here is someone who felt he deserved special treatment because of his hard service and, as a result, cut himself off from receiving the warmth of the father's love, being content to see him merely as an employer. This is the tragedy which lies at the heart of this parable: the one who was closest to his father in proximity was the furthest away from him in intimacy. Here is another expression of human perversity. Not only do we display our rebellion in distancing ourselves from God by flagrantly defying his laws, like the younger son, but we can also distance ourselves from God by hiding behind his laws, like the elder son. Religion can be the most effective way of keeping God at arm's length and ensuring we are in control, just as we see here in the older brother a picture of the Pharisee who came to criticise Jesus. The father wants a loving relationship, the older son wants a business partnership. Why? Presumably so that he can call his father to account when he feels his father fails to keep his side of the bargain. That is the religion of the Pharisee who stands, criticising Jesus and which is still alive today. Here God is not seen as someone with whom we have a personal relationship based upon mercy, but a dutiful partnership based upon merit. Accordingly, we come to church, we pay our dues, and when judgement day comes, we expect God to pay up. Not so, says Jesus. The older son is to enter the party on the same basis as the younger son—at the free, gracious invitation of the father.

Whether you are irreligious and perverse like the younger son, or religious and proud like the older son, God's forgiving love is wide open to us all. We know that because the Son telling this story goes to the cross just a few days afterwards to die for moral and immoral people alike. Those arms stretched wide on that cross symbolise the all-embracing nature of his death. But, as with any relationship, it has to be entered into. You can be like the older son, cutting off your nose to spite your face and forever complaining and staying outside. Or you can be like the younger son, and feel the tender embrace and kiss of the father, and enjoy the party.

8

Faith from Unexpected Prayers

Luke 18: 1–8

The Sunday School class had been studying the story in Matthew 2 where an angel tells Joseph to take his family from Palestine to Egypt to escape the evil clutches of King Herod. One young boy was asked to draw the story of the family's flight into Egypt, so he got his pen and paper out and began to draw a picture of a huge aeroplane. When the teacher saw this, she asked the boy: 'What are you drawing?' Pointing to the aeroplane and three figures seated in the passenger compartment, he said: 'I'm drawing the flight into Egypt.' Then, noticing a shadowy figure in the cockpit, the teacher again asked the boy: 'And who is that in the cockpit?' Getting exasperated by all these annoying questions, he replied frustratedly: 'Well it's obvious isn't it? It's Pontius Pilate!'

Misunderstandings are all too common when it comes to the Christian faith, and perhaps none more so than in the area of prayer. Even for many Christians, prayer is something of a mystery; many of us would say that prayer is a frequent cause of struggle in our Christian lives. Sermons about prayer and books on prayer often leave us feeling guilty and inadequate, partly because the message we often hear is 'pray more'. So we pray more, but we find it harder than ever. We read another book to help us do it, and that spurs us on for a while, but the same old struggles come back. Prayer is often just hard work for the Christian, however much we might say that knowing God is a joy and privilege. Moreover, when we read the stories of Christians of old, they don't offer up much encouragement. George Whitefield, who went to bed punctually at 10 p.m. every night, rose equally promptly at 4 a.m. to pray. It was Martin Luther who said, 'If I fail to spend two hours in prayer each morning, the devil gets the victory through the day. I have so much business I cannot get on without spending three hours daily in prayer'. They may be great men who we have a lot to learn from, yet such examples often leave us feeling woefully inadequate.

Thankfully, Jesus has a lot more to teach us than simply to pray more. Yes, we will find a serious challenge to pray from Jesus' teaching, but when he gives his challenges he gives good reasons to follow them up. He gets right to the heart of why so many of us struggle when it comes to praying, because Jesus doesn't just beat us with a rod of guilt. Rather, he teaches about the character of God in such a way that a proper knowledge of him will be the best motivation and best reason for us to pray. When we understand how good, kind, and just our God is, then we will see that prayer becomes at the least a joy, and most importantly, as we will see, a mark of our trust and dependency on him.

Before turning to the parable we need to understand the context of where this passage comes, because that will shape our grasp of the passage. From 17: 20 the whole discussion is about the second coming of Jesus. Some Pharisees are quizzing Jesus about the coming Kingdom of God. They want to know exactly when this Kingdom would come. But Jesus will have none of it. Dates do not concern him. He wants to turn the tables and ask them a question. The Pharisees ask: 'When will the kingdom come?' and Jesus asks: 'Are you ready for it when it does come?' Jesus will one day return to rule as God's king, and we need to be ready. On that day there will be complete division in the world: 'I tell you,' says Jesus, 'on that night two people will be in one bed; one will be taken, and the other left! Two women will be grinding grain together; one will be taken and the other left' (17: 34–5). A complete division! Two in the office, two in the classroom, two outside the school gates. One taken, the other left! So the big question here in this section of Luke is this: Who is in and who is out? Who is going to be taken to heaven with Jesus when he comes, and who is going to be left behind for judgement? It is an urgent question. The whole of chapter 18 is taken up with Jesus' answer. Jesus is teaching his disciples the marks of being a member of his kingdom in heaven, that is, the marks of being a Christian. One answer is in 18: 1: 'Then Jesus told his disciples a parable, to show them that they should always pray and not give up'. That is his point. One of the hallmarks of the Christian waiting for Jesus' return is persistent, believing prayer. It is not prayer in itself that makes a Christian distinctive. Everyone prays at some point in their lives at times of stress and difficulty. It was Norman Schwarzkopf, the General who led Gulf War I, who said: 'There are no atheists in a foxhole'. Yes, everyone prays. But the mark of the Christian is persistent prayer; someone who prays and does not give up. Prayer is a sign of believing faith.

UNDERSTAND GOD'S CHARACTER

The first lesson is to understand the nature of God's character. Jesus tells a parable to make his point, which is that we should always pray and not give up. This parable is a legal drama. It is the sort of thing the makers of LA Law would love to get their hands on! There are two characters in the story. Firstly, there is a judge: 'In a certain town there was a judge who neither feared God nor cared about men' (v. 2). This is a judge whose reputation goes before him, because he fails on the two vital ingredients of being a judge. In the Old Testament, being a judge meant you feared God and you loved people. This judge did neither. He neither feared God nor cared about men. Even today behind the bench in a court of law there is a royal crest on the wall with a judicial inscription which reads in French 'Dieu et mon Droit', meaning 'God and my Right'. It is a good inscription to have in a court, because justice is all about God's standards and the individual's needs. That is where the judge ought to be focusing. But not this judge. He would have been in the tabloids all the time for his shockingly harsh judgements. You can imagine the name they would give to him: Judge Dread! Most of the time his decisions would have been referred to the European Courts of Human Rights. This judge, Mr Dread QC was not a good judge.

But there is another character in the story and that is the plaintiff, the widow: 'And there was a widow in that town who kept coming to him with the plea, "Grant me justice against my adversary."' (v. 3). It was a case that had dragged on for years. This widow, defenceless, without income and hope, had been pleading with this judge for ages to get justice from her enemy. That was all she wanted: justice. Not revenge, but justice. The judge refused; she persisted. Imagine the scene. The judge comes into the office bright and early, and his secretary says there is a message for him: 'A Mrs Miggins', says the secretary. 'Says she wants justice!' He sits down at his desk and looks at his emails. Immediately he recognises the email address: Widow@jerusalem.org <mailto:Widow@jerusalem.org> 'Give me justice,' she says. He heads down to Court No. 1 for his first case of the day. Who should he find waiting at the door but Mrs Miggins. 'Give me justice,' she says. Eventually, after a long day, he goes home. His wife greets him and says: 'Hello dear, there's a message from a Mrs Miggins. She says can you give her justice!' Finally, before going upstairs to bed, as he puts the cat outside with the empty milk bottles, who should be waiting at the door, but Mrs Miggins! 'I'll see you in the morning,' he says wearily. That was a fatal thing to say because at 8 a.m. the next day, there she is. The whole thing starts again. She keeps coming to him, says Jesus. But for some time, he refused.

Then events take a sudden turn: 'But finally he said to himself, "Even though I don't fear God or care about men, yet because this widow keeps bothering me, I will see that she gets justice, so that she won't eventually wear me out with her coming!"' (vv. 4–5). At last she gets justice. Why? Not because the judge is nice and just—he admits he neither fears God nor cares about people. Rather, he is so fed up with her that he gives in just to get her off his back. The word translated 'wear me out' (v. 5) literally means to give someone a black eye! She has been giving him a good metaphorical beating, a real verbal lashing. And so, at last, she gets her justice. He may do it for selfish reasons, but, whatever the reason, she gets justice.

What, then, is Jesus' teaching here? Many people misunderstand this parable and think Jesus is drawing a straight comparison between the unjust judge and God. That is precisely what many of us do think about God when it comes to prayer. We think God is like a grumpy old judge who needs to be badgered into giving us what we want. We often fall into the trap of thinking God is like an old snack machine. If you thump it hard enough in a certain place you are bound to get a chocolate. Sometimes, though, the machine will eat your money and give you nothing. But other times you would get the sweets and the money back. Is prayer not like that? A bit of a lottery? Is God not like that? Someone who needs to be harangued into giving what you want?

It is such misunderstanding that leads many of us to struggle in our prayer lives, because we fail to understand to whom we are praying. Jesus is teaching us that the first step to understanding prayer and to being able to pray is to know the God to whom we are praying. The whole point of this parable is not to make a comparison between the judge and God, but to make a contrast. Jesus' argument runs like this: if this nasty judge can give justice to a widow and, moreover, for his own gain, then how much more will a loving, gracious God, such as our God, give good gifts to his spiritual children. That is the point of the parable. (The argument is in the form of *a minore ad maius* construction, a phrase which means 'from the lesser to the greater'.) In the light of that, Jesus says to pray and not to give up. Remember who it is you are praying to!

And so what kind of God are we praying to according to Jesus?

Firstly, we are praying to a God of love. Remember! Judge Dread QC did not care a jot about God or people (v. 4). He only answered out of selfish pride. He was fed up with this widow badgering him all the time. But that is not what God is like at all. Look at what Jesus says in verse 7: 'And will not God bring about justice for his chosen ones who cry out to him day and night? Will he keep putting them off?' God is a God who delights to answer the prayers of his people. He is not going to keep putting them off. Jesus tells us in Luke 11 that God is far better than human fathers, because if human fathers, though evil, know how to give good gifts to their children, how much more does God! God delights to give his children good gifts. He is not going to keep putting them off. The apostle Paul tells us God is 'able to do immeasurably more than all we ask or imagine' (Eph. 3: 20). The God of the Bible is that kind of God. He is not a grumpy old judge who does not want to bother, but rather a delightful, loving Father who wishes to hear and answer the prayers of his children.

By illustration, we might think about the court of Alexander the Great. Among those in the court of Alexander was a philosopher of outstanding ability, but little money. One day he asked Alexander for financial help and was told to draw whatever he needed from the imperial treasury. But when the man requested an amount equal to £50,000 he was refused, as the treasurer needed to verify that such a large sum was authorized. When he asked Alexander, the ruler replied, 'Pay the money at once. The philosopher has done me a singular honour. By the largeness of his request he shows that he has understood both my wealth and generosity.' Do we believe that God is a God of bountiful love, or a grumpy, stingy old judge? The way we pray will reveal what we really think.

Secondly, he is a God of justice: 'And the Lord said: "Listen to what the unjust judge says. And will not God bring about justice for his chosen ones who cry out to him day and night?"' (vv. 6–7). Whereas this judge was unjust, the God of the Bible is a God of impeccable justice. He upholds the cause of the oppressed and will bring about justice for his people. So Jesus says in verse 8: 'I tell you, he will see that they get justice, and quickly.' For many of us this is where we come up against a problem, because sometimes we find there is no quick answer. It seems to be taking God an age to answer our prayers. It may well be that you are going through a difficult time in your life and you have been faithful in prayer; you have laid before the Lord all your cares and worries as the Bible tells you, but still there is no answer. It seems as if the heavens are bronze. God seems to be silent and feels so distant. What then? The answer to that question is in the context of the passage because Jesus is talking about his Second Coming. He is pointing us forward and telling us it is that time which is the final balancing of the books. When Jesus returns, then his justice will be swift and final. It will be like the days of Noah, or the days of Sodom and Gomorrah, when God's judgement was executed swiftly and suddenly. Yes, there will be justice, but the final balancing of the books will not be until Jesus returns. If you think God is like the unjust judge then you will stop praying in the meantime, but Jesus tells this parable to teach us to pray and not give up; literally, not to grow weary of praying. That is why he teaches us about the character of God. This parable does not teach everything there is to know about prayer, and sometimes we might go through terrible difficulty and pain in our lives where there appears to be no answer from heaven, but God is just and loving. He will act in judgement swiftly when Jesus returns. If we give up believing in a God who is powerful and good enough to vindicate his people and act in judgement, then we will stop praying in the meantime. Jesus tells us not to because of the character of God.

REMEMBER YOUR STATUS

There is another lesson, however, that Jesus has to teach us and that is to remember our status. Once again there is a contrast, not a comparison, between the widow and us.

Widows in Jesus' day were extremely vulnerable. More often than not they were young widows, since husbands often died young. But when the husband died, the breadwinner of the family went too. The widow would have no income, and, in the days before Social Security and benefits, she would be weak and vulnerable. They were helpless, hopeless, and loveless, especially if they had no family to look after them. The early Christians went to great lengths to protect the widows in their congregations. The church was their social security. So for this poor widow in Jesus' story, she would have had no husband to defend her, no money to pay the judge, no one to lean on the judge or bribe him. All she could do was use 'pester power' to get justice.

Jesus' point is this: if this helpless, hopeless, and loveless widow eventually got justice, then how much more will we? How can we be sure though? What is so different about us? It is because of what Jesus calls us as God's people in verse 7. He says we are the 'chosen ones'. Christians have been adopted into God's family on his initiative and under his guiding care and hand to be his children. If that is the case, then how much more should we approach the throne of grace and keep on praying as Jesus tells us to. If this helpless widow persisted in her requests to the unjust judge, how much more should we persist in prayer to the just and loving judge of all the world? Indeed, how much more so when we can call that just judge, Father? How much more does our loving God and Father delight over us, his children, whom he has personally adopted and chosen for his family? When we pray, we are enjoying a special privilege reserved for the precious children of God. How God delights and treasures us! What is more, how he longs to hear his children praying to him, for we are his chosen ones. Not poor widows, but his precious children, saved by his Son's blood.

When you know the Father, you can have access to him at any time. The story is told of an American soldier who wanted to get compassionate leave so he could care for his dying mother. He tried to get permission but failed, so he decided to go straight to the top. It was in the days of Abraham Lincoln's presidency, and the soldier went boldly up to the White House, but was told that it was impossible to see the President. He went away sad. As he sat dejected in the park, a little boy came up to him and asked what was wrong. So the soldier told his story, and at the end of his tale the little boy said: 'Follow me'. So they went back up the White House drive through the doors, down a corridor and through another door into where President Lincoln himself was sitting. When Lincoln saw his young son, he said: 'What is it Todd?' The little boy replied, 'Father, there is a man here who wants to speak to you. Please would you listen to him?'

If you think entry to a human king or president is awesome enough, then how about to the King of Kings? Yet so often we ignore and forget just who we are in God's eyes. But if we forget our status before God, a chosen adopted child of God by his grace, then we will give up praying for sure. So let us remember our status. We are precious children of God adopted by grace.

HEAR JESUS' CHALLENGE

Finally, we must hear Jesus' challenge. Jesus ends with a sting in the tail as so often at the end of his parables.

So far he has taught us about the character of God, how he is not like the unjust judge, but rather is just and loving. He has also taught us about our status as his chosen and loved children. What, then, would you expect Jesus to say at the end of this parable? Probably something like: 'So keep praying and don't give up!' After all, he has told us in verse 1 to always pray and not give up! But that is not how Jesus finished: 'However, when the Son of Man comes, will he find faith on the earth?' (v. 8).

What does Jesus mean? It must be related to all that he has said before. What he is asking is whether, when he returns, he will find his people praying persistently, exercising their faith and trust in their just judge and heavenly father? Or, when he returns, will he find that his people have given up being faithful and stopped trusting God? In effect, he is saying that persistent, believing prayer is a mark of true, believing faith. Prayer does not get us into heaven, but it shows where we place our confidence, namely, in God and not ourselves.

Believing persistent prayer is a mark of the genuine Christian. It is not going to be easy to remain faithful in these last days before Jesus returns. We can assume this because Jesus telling us not to give up indicates that the temptation to give up will be strong. Yet, Jesus does not want quitters—he wants those who will persevere; who will keep praying for justice to be done, for God's kingdom to be finally and fully established, and for God's glory to be seen in the world. He wants people who will keep looking forward to that great day when Jesus returns. He wants people of faith; people who trust the promises of God.

Of course, we might be tempted to say, 'Well it hasn't happened for two thousand years! Is it really going to happen?' That is exactly what people thought in Noah's day: 'Just as it was in the days of Noah, so also will it be in the days of the Son of Man' (Luke 17: 26). No one believed Noah. And what happened? 'Then the flood came and destroyed them all!' (17: 27). Will Jesus really break his promise? Another temptation is simply to get sucked into living life in this world, working, holidaying, building, buying, eating, and drinking. Too busy really to think about the return of Jesus or to live a life dedicated to God's ways? That is what happened in Sodom. And what happened there? 'Fire and sulphur rained down from heaven and destroyed them all' (17: 29). Do not be fooled. Jesus will return. The question is how will he find us?

9

A Call with an Unexpected Demand

Luke 14: 25-35

We are often reminded that we live in the age of the 'sound-bite'. No matter how complex the issue or how tremendous the implications, to communicate something effectively, it has to be reduced to a short, pithy, memorable statement. This is nothing new. Advertising men or spin doctors may have taken it to new levels of sophistication, but the catchy, punchy line or two has always had the power to make an impact. That is the attraction of graffiti: 'Dyslexia rules—KO', 'Apathy rules—O'. One of my favourites is: 'To do is to be—Plato. To be is to do—Aristotle. Do be, do be do—Sinatra.' In this chapter we look at some sound-bites that surround two parables of Jesus, which spell out what it means to be a Christian, and, as we shall see, it is all a matter of what we do as Christians.

THE CALL TO BE COMMITTED

> Large crowds were travelling with Jesus, and turning to them he said: 'If anyone comes to me and does not hate his father and mother, his wife and children, his brothers and sisters—yes, even his own life—he cannot

be my disciple. And anyone who does not carry his cross and follow me cannot be my disciple.'

vv. 25–6

Notice what is happening and what Jesus does. It is enough to cause many modern-day evangelists to cough out their dentures in horror. Large crowds are following him. Here we have the literal fulfilment of the parable which has just gone before with its climax in verse 23: 'Go out to the roads and country lanes and make them come in, so that my house will be full.' It is already happening and here they are en mass. So what does Jesus do? Climb a soapbox and give a speech to rouse the troops? Pump up the volume on the amp and whip up the crowd into a religious frenzy? Hardly! He stops them dead in their tracks and delivers two rabbit punch sound-bites which are enough to make anyone think twice about going any further.

First, there is the demand that we put Christ before others: 'If anyone comes to me and does not hate his father and mother, his wife and children, his brothers and sisters—yes, even his own life—he cannot be my disciple' (v. 26). That is strong stuff. 'If you do not hate those closest to you then you cannot be my follower.' That is what the text says. But what does the text mean? It means this: that if we do not love Jesus in such a way that our love for our nearest and dearest does not appear to be hatred in comparison, then we cannot be one of his people. Allegiance and devotion to him is to be the sort of allegiance and devotion you would normally reserve for God—because he is God. That is the implication. Remember the two great commandments? 'Love the Lord your God with all your heart and with all your soul and with all your strength and with all your mind', then 'Love your neighbour as yourself' (Luke 10: 27). Get those in the wrong order and you have idolatry. The twentieth century was the century of the second commandment—putting man above God, worshipping humanity rather than the one who made humanity. Invariably, with that you end up killing humanity, for there is no fear of God to stop you. Sadly, the church has followed suit—promoting the pleasing of man rather than the pleasing of God. How much Christian work has been stifled because the wife would not approve, so the extra money goes on the kitchen rather than for the gospel? Or because the children do not approve—'We want Sundays for other things: our sport, our horse-riding, our parties'—so whole families are kept away from Christian service. But we rationalise it—we do not want to make Christianity too hard in case it puts them off, and so we make it 'convenient'. But that is not what Jesus says here. A middle-aged couple became Christians later in life, much to the acute embarrassment of their grown-up offspring. They were given an ultimatum: the children said, 'Mum, Dad, it is either us or Christianity. Which is it going to be?' They chose Christ and they have neither seen nor spoken to their children since. That is heartbreaking, but it is what Jesus means by sound-bite one.

Sound-bite two: 'Anyone who does not carry his cross and follow me cannot be my disciple' (v. 26). This is the demand to put Christ before self. That is what this business about carrying a cross means. To carry a cross was a public statement that the one shouldering it was to be impaled upon it. In other words, he was to die. To these people, Jesus could not have been more offensive had he told them, as Jews, to bathe in pig's blood. The cross was normally reserved for radicals, revolutionaries; those who foolishly chose to go against the might of the Roman Empire. But, of course, that is exactly what Jesus was doing. Here is Jesus the revolutionary, but we have turned him into Jesus the entertainer. His followers are meant to go against the flow.

Such talk of cross-carrying is just as offensive to our self-absorbed, self-therapeutic society now as it was to Jesus' society then. One secular counsellor has listed thirty-seven 'rights' we should all enjoy; amongst them are the following: 'I have a right to dignity and respect. I have a right to make decisions based on my feelings, my judgement, or any reason I should choose. I have a right to be happy.' Jesus says, 'No you don't, not if you are going to be a follower of mine—I now claim those rights.' Jesus is emphatic about it. You 'cannot be my disciple' without doing this. There is this no-nonsense, 'all or nothing' nature about these kingdom sound-bites. The problem is we want to bargain with Jesus and tone down the nature of his demands, or turn them on their head altogether to make them more palatable. We want to talk about Christianity being 'cool', whilst Jesus talks about Christianity involving a cross. A former Anglican minister who became a Buddhist, Alan Watts, puts his finger on the issue when he writes, 'Without any disrespect it must be said that Christianity is pre-eminently the gambler's religion. In no other religion are the stakes so high and the choice so momentous.' Jesus is not playing games here. He is wanting us—body, mind, and soul. He wants us to gamble everything on him. So we had better know what we are letting ourselves in for, which is the point of these two parables which amplify the sound-bites.

A CALL TO BE WISE

The first parable is something many of his followers would be able to identify with. Just imagine you want to build a tower on your farm for storage purposes, that is the picture Jesus uses in verse 28. The first thing you will do is a feasibility study. You will get an architect who will cost you an arm and a leg. Then you will get an accountant (another arm gone!) and work out the total costs involved, and only then will you begin building. What you do not do is have a grandiose scheme, call the workmen to lay the foundation and perhaps a few bricks on top of that, only to find you cannot complete the job. All you would be left with would be a monument to your own stupidity—what used to be called a 'folly'. In a shame culture like the one Jesus is addressing (v. 29), you would avoid that like the plague. In other words, Jesus is saying, 'Count the cost.' There is a cost in following Jesus. Our difficulty is that we live in a credit culture, where we take all the benefits now and put off footing the bill until much later, or, better still, let someone else pick it up. That is something which can easily be transferred into Christianity. Expectations are raised that being a Christian will be 'all blessing with minimum difficulty'. The swipe card of prayer is used and instant answers are called for, usually centred on ourselves. That is not the way Jesus presents it here. There is no credit, it is cash-on-demand, up front. You must ensure you have what it takes to follow him. So be thoughtful, says Jesus.

The second parable raises the stakes even higher, for here is a king preparing to go to war. More than reputation is at stake, it is peoples' lives (vv. 31–2). A wise king will make sure he can win. If it looks like he does not have the resources to counter a foe with a 2:1 advantage, then he will take the diplomatic route if he has any sense. He will use his brain before making such an important decision of committing his country to war. All that sounds very familiar. But there is an additional point here. Not only must potential followers of Christ be thoughtful, they must be decisive. It will not do for a ruler in a war situation to dilly-dally in making decisions. That is why during the Second World War, Chamberlain, the appeasement Prime Minister, had to go, and Churchill, the warrior, had to be brought in. Too much was at stake.

Someone once said that he was going to buy the book *The Power of Positive Thinking*, and then thought, 'What's the point?' Indecisiveness can be a snare, especially when it comes to matters of eternity. It could well be that is where you are. You have heard the claims of Jesus, you know your eternal destiny depends upon responding to him, you are even willing to follow at a distance mingling in the crowd. This same Jesus is stopping and turning to you and challenging you to make a decision. Either follow him and have the courage of your convictions or walk away from him and stop wasting his time.

Then again, you may be an enthusiast at the front of the crowd, but if the truth be known you feel a little uncomfortable with verse 33, which sums up everything Jesus has been saying so far: 'Any of you who does not give up everything he has cannot be my disciple.' The test of whether we are taking these words of Jesus seriously is how we follow him in the daily routine of life. It was the great Christian writer Oswald Chambers who pointed out that 'drudgery is the touchstone of Christian character.' Think about that. He writes:

> Walking on the water is easy to impulsive pluck, but walking on dry land as a disciple of Jesus Christ is a different thing. Peter walked on the water to go to Jesus, but he followed him afar off on land. We do not need the grace of God to stand crises, human nature and pride are sufficient, we can face the strain magnificently; but it does require the supernatural grace of God to live 24 hours in every day as a saint, to go through drudgery as a disciple, to live an ordinary, unobserved, ignored existence as a disciple of Jesus. It is inbred in us that we have to do exceptional things for God; but we have not. We have to be exceptional in the ordinary things, to be holy in mean streets, among mean people, and this is not learned in five minutes.

So the question is this: Are you a 24/7 Christian or only when it suits? It was John Newton who once said to a Christian who was moaning about not feeling like doing anything and that it was proving too difficult following Jesus: 'Don't tell me of your feelings. A traveller would be glad of fine weather, but if he is a man of business he will go on.' That is precisely what Jesus is looking for in you and me.

That tone of Newton could well be capturing the tone of Jesus, such that what he really is doing is motivating people to follow him by raising the bar rather than turning people away. Think of it like this. You have an athletics coach who at the first session typically gives the team members a pep talk. The coach lays it on the line that he or she expects to see everyone turn up for the training sessions on time, to give one hundred per cent, to give up anything that will prevent them from giving of their best. He wants the best from the best. And then comes the line in deadly earnest: 'OK, if you are not willing to do this then go now, you are not worthy to wear the uniform.' You could slink out at that point, to the ridicule of your team-mates (parable one), but you have signed on with both eyes wide open; you have made your decision and you are going to stay (parable two). Christianity is not for quitters. It requires more courage to be a Christian than it does to be a non-Christian because anyone can be big and mindless in a crowd. The Christian, however, has to be twice as sharp and twice as courageous. But of course he is not alone, he has Jesus. Notice that Jesus talks about being 'my disciple'. We are not committed to a programme or even a movement, but to a person, and this is the one person we can rely on.

What is it that is going to be so costly in following Jesus? To some extent we have already come across the answer and it is brought to a head in verse 34.

A CALL TO BE DIFFERENT

'Salt is good, but if it loses its saltiness, how can it be made salty again? It is fit neither for the soil nor for the manure heap; it is thrown out' (v. 34). While our attitudes and behaviour are not that different from those around us we will not have much hassle. It is because we do not wish to upset our parents or spouse or children that we will be tempted to soften and dilute our faith. The reason we want to get along with them is because we are concerned about our own well-being, our self, and that is why Jesus says that has to be crucified if we are going to be his disciples. This is the point about this third sound-bite about salt. It has nothing to do with being rubbed into society as a preservative, because here its main function is as a component of compost—

manure—and salt which can no longer be distinguished as salt, is not even good for that.

How should the followers of Jesus be distinctive and so draw both the opposition and interest of a world on the run from God? The way our distinctiveness will work out will depend upon where we are as a society: it is all relative. If Christianity is a matter of being properly related to God, and living life as God intends it to be lived, and if one of the main features of our fallen world is that it goes off in different directions at different times, then in wanting to live a balanced life the Christian pulls away from society at the particular point at which it finds itself rebelling against God. Let us illustrate.

In a society sold on sexual gratification, as ours is, the Christian will emphasise chastity: sex is for heterosexual marriage, full stop. That will make Christians stand out and attract all the taunts and barbed comments. The Christian girl who cherishes her chastity at university will be made to feel subnormal, no matter what the rhetoric about a woman's right to choose. That is the way it will go. On the other hand, if a Christian finds himself in a society that downgrades sex as something evil but necessary (such societies have existed in the past), then the Christian will stress the wonder of sex as one of God's most precious and powerful gifts to be cherished and celebrated.

Let us take another example. We live in a society that emphasises emotions above thinking: 'if it feels good, do it.' The more mindless the entertainment the better, and now we have drugs to help us lose ourselves more than ever before, alongside sophisticated technology now widely available. In those situations, it is disastrous for Christians to Christianise such trends. Then worship events become little more than an alternative version of what the non-Christian is doing anyway, with the only difference being that we add 'God words' to the songs. Then we are not being distinctive. In that situation, the Christian will be counter-cultural by underlining the use of the mind. In a culture where books are not read, the Christian will read books, because Christianity, if it is nothing else, is a religion of the Word. He will not lose sight of the place of the emotions, but relative to his culture he will appear odd for wanting to make decisions based on careful thought and argument arising out of God's Word rather than on self-centred emotions. Conversely, in a culture where the dominance is on cold analysis and the reign of science, the Christian will remind people that we are more than thinking-machines; we are made with hearts of flesh, we feel as well as think. Do you see how it works? Emphasise that Jesus is the only way to God and you will be accused of intolerance, even though we defend the right for anyone to hold whatever views they wish. Stress that all we need to know of God and how to live properly in his world is found in the Bible and you will be called a fundamentalist. Show joy and emotion in a church service and you will be written off as 'happy-clappy'. Preach the Bible for more than twenty-five minutes and you will be hounded as cerebral and intellectual. That is how it goes. Jesus was accused of being a drunkard and glutton because he did not conform to the tight religious standards of his day. He was also accused of being demon-possessed when he was more strict in applying the Scriptures than the religious elite. If we are going to follow Jesus at this point we can expect to draw the same flak. From the viewpoint of the world, Christians are always in a 'lose-lose' situation. But not from God's viewpoint, the only viewpoint that matters—eternity. 'He who has ears to hear, let him hear.'

10

The Shock of Grace

Matthew 20: 1-16

'Love and scandal are the best sweeteners of tea.' So wrote the eighteenth century English author, Henry Fielding. If you were to cast your eye over the tabloid headlines on any given day, you would be right in thinking that we in Britain are obsessed with scandals. One particular scandal that we love is the royal scandal. These get the papers excited. Paul Burrell, the former butler of Princess Diana, was accused of stealing thousands of items from her house. Before that, it was Princess Anne's dog which allegedly attacked some innocent passer-by in Windsor Great Park. Yes, royal scandals really get us excited.

In Matthew 20, however, we discover a royal scandal with a difference. This scandal is in the royal kingdom of God. Indeed, the scandal goes right to the heart of the heavenly government; right to the top, right to the King of kings, God himself. It is a scandal with God at the centre. The reason this scandal comes to light is because Jesus speaks about it through one of his parables. It is a story the Confederation of British Industry or the Trades Union Congress would not be happy with. They would not have had Jesus preaching at one of their conferences with this scandal attached to him.

Jesus tells the story of a landowner who has a shocking way of paying his workers. He says that if you work for one hour, then you get the same as the person who has worked for twelve hours. That is scandalous! But Jesus is insistent in verse 1 that the kingdom of heaven is like this. He is teaching something about God's priorities and actions. When we set this in the wider context of the passage as a whole, we find out that Jesus is illustrating a shocking principle. In Matthew 19: 30, Jesus says: 'But many who are first will be last, and many who are last will be first'. And then, in Matthew 20: 1 he says, 'For, the kingdom of heaven is like a landowner....'. This parable illustrates the point of 19: 29, and, at the end of the story, Jesus says: 'So the last will be first and the first will be last' (20: 16).

So what does this little phrase, which has come into common speaking today, mean? What is it about this phrase that Jesus illustrates in our parable? What Jesus is saying is that the way God thinks and the way God acts are often different from the way the world acts and thinks. The kingdom of God has a different way of looking at things to how we do. It is an upside-down kingdom. In the previous passage, a rich young man has been turned away from Jesus because he is unwilling to give himself wholeheartedly to Jesus. The disciples understandably ask in 19: 25: 'Who then can be saved?' Jesus replies, 'With man it is impossible, but with God all things are possible.' With God it is possible for country fishermen to know God personally. With God it is possible for children who seem least useful in the world to come into the kingdom. God's kingdom is a kingdom where the world's values are turned on their head. It is not a matter of power and prestige and moral virtue. His kingdom is about a simple childlike trust in God, which takes no account of power, influence, and prestige in this world. God's kingdom is a topsy-turvy kingdom and, no matter where you stand in the world's pegging, with God there is a level playing field.

This parable is about how we get into the kingdom of God; what criteria God has for entry into his kingdom. Jesus tells this parable to illustrate that point, and he does it for two reasons. Firstly, he is wanting to remind the disciples of God's upside-down principles, so that they who have surrendered their lives to God will receive generously from him. They should, however, also be wary of being smug, because in God's kingdom, he is generous to others whom the world might think do not deserve such generosity, and there is no room for envy. Like all of Jesus' parables, this one comes with a sting in the tale. This one is designed to shock, and there are two shocks in store for us.

THE SHOCK OF GOD'S SOVEREIGN CHOICE

Firstly, there is the shock of God's sovereign choice, which we see in the first half of the parable as the landowner recruits the workers. Picture the scene: it is 6 a.m. at the Chateau Bethlehemberg vineyards. The landowner knows the time has come to pick the grapes for the AD 33 vintage and he needs hired men to do his work. Maybe he has heard from the Jerusalem weather centre that storms are on the way. Whatever the reason, the work needs to be done today, so he goes down to the job centre, which is the local market. There, men would gather who needed work and who hoped to be hired for the day so that they could put some food on the table for their families. Sure enough, the landowner finds a bunch of workers. They agree on a fee for the day: one denarius, the standard working fee for the day, then sign the contracts and off they go. Everyone is happy.

But at the third hour, which is 9 a.m., the landowner goes out again and finds more men doing nothing in the market place waiting to be hired. So he says to them: 'You also go and work in my vineyard and I will pay you whatever is right' (v. 4). So off they went to work. The landowner quotes no specific price. He simply says that he will pay them what is right. I guess if they knew that a whole day's work is one denarius, then they would work it out that they would receive about three quarters of a denarius. That would only seem fair.

The landowner's recruiting drive does not stop there, however. He goes out again at the sixth and the ninth hour, about midday, when half the day has gone, and then again at 3 p.m. when the day is nearly over. Still he is looking for workers, and we begin to wonder: 'Well, hasn't this landowner made a mistake. He's been to the job centre four times now, and still he hasn't got enough workers. Surely he's made a management error, hasn't he?' But Jesus makes it clear in this parable that the landowner's trips to the job centre stem not from a bad dose of mismanagement, but rather from a remarkable concern for the needs of these workers, because the final trip the landowner makes is at the eleventh hour, that is about five in the afternoon. There is just one hour's work left. Eleven twelfths of the working day have gone. But still the landowner is out there. Why? Verses 6–7 give the reason: 'About the eleventh hour, he went out and found still others standing around. He asked them: "Why have you been standing here all day long doing nothing?" "Because no-one has hired us," they answered. He said to them: "You also go and work in my vineyard."' This landowner is concerned for these workers. They have been standing there all day, not through idleness, but because there is no work. So what is his reason for hiring them? They are unemployed. He knows he is not going to get much out of them. They are hardly going to do an hour's work before the day is over. But such is the compassion and generosity of the landowner that he is so bothered about their employment.

If this landowner had not come down to the market place and seen these men, had he not come down five times during the day, then many men would have been without a wage. Many would have gone hungry, because that was the way society worked then. If you did not work, you did not get paid, so you did not eat. It was all because of the generosity and the kindness of the landowner that these men got work. It was his free choice.

The first shock that Jesus is teaching us from this parable, then, is the shock of God's sovereign choice. In this story, the landowner is God. That is often the way in Jesus' parables. The scandal of this first part of the parable is that the only way we can get into heaven is through God's sovereign choice. He chooses out of his incredible love to save his people; to bring people into his kingdom. But it is all his doing. So everyone in heaven is there because God brought them there. If the landowner had not come down to the market place then no one in that village would be working that day. They would have faced a day without work, without pay, and without food. Equally, if God had not acted to rescue us, then we would face a far more serious fate. We would not be without work; we would be outside the kingdom facing judgement day on our own. We would not be without pay; we would be without salvation.

This is the plain teaching of the Bible. Ephesians 2 tells us we are dead in our transgressions and sins. Now there is no way in the world that a dead body can raise itself, and there is no way in the world that a spiritually dead person can bring themselves back to life. Time and again we hear the same message: God is the one who takes the initiative to save us. We cannot take it ourselves. He decides to save us. And we will be in heaven because of his sovereign choice.

This cuts right across what the world says. The world says we can decide our own futures, we can make of our lives what we want; the Bible says we cannot do that spiritually. God alone is powerful enough to take the initiative to save spiritually dead people like you and me. Often this worldly attitude creeps into our Christian language. We say that we found Jesus. We say that we decided for Christ. Now, of course, there is some truth in that. God's sovereign choice does not mean we are mere robots. No, we are responsible for receiving his offer of salvation. We are responsible for how we respond to him. But he opens our eyes to see the truth. He brings us to the point where we can decide. The fact is that he found us.

A well-known evangelist tells the story of when he went to speak to a particular school with an audience of A Level students. The evangelist was saying that none of them could become Christians unless God took the initiative. Now, as with some A Level students, one young man thought he knew better than the evangelist and he said: 'Oh, that's rubbish. I could become a Christian whenever I wanted to.' So the evangelist said: 'OK. Prove it. Give us a demonstration now. Become a Christian'. 'No,' said the boy, 'I don't want to.' 'Well, want to want to,' said the evangelist. 'Show me I'm wrong.' 'No I don't want to.' After a while going back and forth, the evangelist said: 'You can't can you.' And the boy said very quietly: 'No, I can't.'

That is the shock of God's sovereign choice. He has to take the initiative to rescue us. That has two lessons for us. Firstly, it means we must be humble; we must remember we cannot save ourselves. Only God can, and that should humble us. It is humbling for the Christian because it means we realise we can do nothing to save ourselves and our pride is broken. But it is humbling too for those who are not yet Christians, because it reminds them too that there is nothing they can do to revive themselves spiritually. By nature we are dead in our sins. Only God can save us.

Secondly, it means we should be grateful. We should thank God every day that he took the initiative to bring us into his kingdom to rescue us. For without him coming to rescue us, we would be lost. Humility and gratitude. Those are the responses to the first shock in this parable, that of God's sovereign choice.

THE SHOCK OF GOD'S EXTRAVAGANT GENEROSITY

There is a second shock Jesus wishes to teach in this parable, and that is the shock of God's extravagant generosity, which we see in the second half of the parable (vv. 8–16).

Let us return to Jesus' story. The day has ended and it is pay time. The landowner asks his foreman to get the workers together and pay them: 'Call the workers and pay them their wages, beginning with the last ones hired and going on to the first' (v. 8). What follows is extraordinary. One Bible translator has called this parable the story of the eccentric employer. It looks strange to our eyes. The last are paid first and the landowner says that they are to receive one denarius, a day's pay for an hour's work. It is incredible generosity, and no doubt these men rub their hands with glee. What a wonderful employer! They have got twelve times what they deserve. When it comes to the rest of the field, everyone else is no doubt doing a few hasty calculations. You can almost see the pound signs come up in their eyes. You can hear the cash registers ringing in their minds. 'Ah', say the first group who have worked for twelve hours. 'If the last lot got one denarius, then we'll get twelve times as much.' That is twelve denarii. Even the dimmest of them could have worked that out!

But what happens? 'So when those came who were hired first, they expected to receive more. But each one of them also received a denarius' (v. 10). They were furious and begin to grumble against the landowner. The rep for the National Union of Vinedressers comes to the landowner and says: 'These men who were hired last worked only one hour and you have made them equal to us who have borne the burden of the work and the heat of the day' (v. 12). But do you see what the landowner says: 'Friend, I am not being unfair to you. Didn't you agree to work for a denarius? Take your pay and go. I want to give the man I hired last the same as I gave you. Don't I have the right to do what I want with my money? Or are you envious because I am so generous?' (v. 13). This landowner is not unfair to these workers. They signed the contract. They got what they deserved. What they could not stomach was the incredible generosity of the landowner.

That is the real shock of this parable. The shock is seen in what the men hired first say to the landowner. You made them equal to us, they say. And that is precisely the point. This parable is not about how God treats his workers who work for him. Other parables show how God rewards faithfulness in the kingdom. This parable is about God's generosity in allowing people into his kingdom where the first are last and the last first. The values of the world are turned completely on their head. The world says the more you do, the more you deserve. The trouble is we think that carries over with God's values. The more we do to impress God, the more he will give us. The more we go to church, the more we give, the longer we serve on a committee, the less we swear, and the less we cheat people, the more God will be impressed. 'Surely he'll be impressed and let us into heaven? Surely all those things will get us up the ladder with God?' When it comes to getting into heaven, none of that can help. None of us can get into heaven on our own merits. None of us deserve heaven, no matter how good we have been. We all fall short of God's perfect standards. We deserve just the opposite of heaven: hell. The only way we can get into heaven is if God lets us in. Getting into heaven is all about his generosity. That is the shock of this parable. Grace is the great leveller. The first shall be last and the last first. In the race to heaven, we all cross the line at the same time. The only way we can get into heaven is by trusting and receiving God's gracious gift. And the shock is that God is willing to be generous to people you and I would never dream of being generous to; the last in our world.

What is it that is so shocking about Jeffrey Dahmer? It is not his acts, though they are horrible. Jeffrey Dahmer was convicted on a count of seventeen murders, all of which were carried out in the most horrific fashion. This man was a cannibal, and was called the Milwaukee Monster. It is not that the trial was the most shocking thing, even though Dahmer sat serenely through the whole thing, with not even a glimmer of remorse on his face. Nor is his punishment such a shock. Life imprisonment, though life would hardly do for even one of the murders he committed. What is so shocking about Jeffrey Dahmer is his conversion. Months before a fellow inmate murdered him, Dahmer became a Christian. He said he was profoundly sorry for what he had done. He said he put his faith in Christ. He said he wanted a fresh start. That is what most people find shocking. It is that when we get to heaven, we will be side by side with this horrific cannibal, worshipping together our saviour and Lord. He will be our brother in Christ. That is shocking! Yet what is perhaps more sobering to realise is that we have no more reason to be in heaven than Dahmer does. We are there because of God's extravagant generosity. That is the shocking thing about God's grace. God is willing to give his grace to those we would never dream of giving it to.

It is not as if God has forgotten Dahmer's crimes. Do you think God has just swept all those seventeen murders under the carpet? No. How can God allow someone like Jeffrey Dahmer into heaven? Because his crimes have been paid for by someone else. Someone else has taken all that injustice on his shoulders and borne the price of those murders. That someone is Jesus Christ. When Jesus died on the cross, he took Jeffrey Dahmer's sin, and paid the price so that he could go to heaven. How is it that a filthy sinner, or perhaps a respectable sinner, can get into heaven? Because Jesus died on the cross for them. Such generosity is not cheap. It comes at a huge price: the death of God's own son. That is why in heaven there will be teachers, doctors, vicars, and lawyers, people the world may respect, rubbing shoulders with murderers, prostitutes, armed burglars, and muggers, whom the world hates. The first will be last, the last first. Everyone there will be there because of God's extravagant generosity. All as forgiven sinners. Is it not a shocking thought that Billy Graham and Jeffrey Dahmer will both be in heaven? That is the shock of extravagant generosity.

There are two other important lessons for us in the shock of God's extravagant generosity. The first is to never think that we are superior to other Christians. If grace is the great leveller, if we all cross the finishing line at the same time, then there is no place in the church for a superior attitude. We have no right to look down our noses at other Christians and question God as to why they are in church. What right do we have to do that? What right do we have to ask God why he gives his grace to some people who we would not include? Like those first workers, we are in danger of calling God unfair. Yet nothing could be further from the truth. If it was not for the landowner, no one would be working that day. And if it was not for God's grace, none of us would be heading for heaven. Do not be superior. It is easy to do, even subconsciously, as we compare ourselves with others. As soon as we do it, we forget how gracious God has been to us, and we show ourselves not to have fully grasped how wonderfully generous he is.

The second application is not to think that we are inferior. All too often it is easy for some Christians to fall into this second trap: to think God is not interested in us; to think that somehow everyone else is better than us; to think we do not come up to everyone else's standards. Maybe you have sinned in a way of which you are deeply ashamed. Well, remember how generous God is; he will forgive every sin if you come to him. Do not think you are inferior. In God's eyes, you are precious. He sent his Son to die for you. Nothing could show you how God feels about you more than that.

There is the true story about a young girl in Brazil named Christina. She lived in the country with her Mum, and, like many young people, she wanted to experience the high-life of the city. So, early one morning, she gathered her things together, left the house and her Mum and went straight for the city. When her mother awoke later that morning she was devastated. She knew her daughter had been thinking about it, but never thought she would leave. So she bought a return ticket and set off straightaway to the big city. When she got there, she photocopied a photograph of herself and put a message on the back. She then placed the photo in all the bars and clubs she could find, went back home and waited. Some time later, Christina was in one of those bars and happened to see a dog-eared photo of her Mum behind the bar. She took it down and turned it over and on the back were these words: 'Wherever you are, whatever you've done, come home!' And she did just that. That is a picture of the shock of God's extravagant generosity; that he can say to us: 'Wherever you are, whatever you've done, come home!' He will have you back if you will have him. That is the kind of God he is.

11

Spurned Love

Matthew 21: 33–46

There seems to be no limit to the lengths to which people will go to be rulers of their own little world. Take the well-known atheist Aldous Huxley the author of *Brave New World*. What made this great intellectual an atheist? Was it that his razor-sharp mind ruled out the possibility that there was a God? Was it that the arguments against God's existence stacked up more favourably than the arguments for? Not according to his own confession. This is what he wrote as to why he wanted the world to be, in reality, meaningless: 'For myself, no doubt, as for many of my contemporaries, the philosophy of meaninglessness was essentially liberation from a certain political and economic system and liberation from a certain system of morality. We objected to the morality because it interfered with our sexual freedom'. In my experience as a minister, that is what I have often found. The reason many people claim they do not believe in God is because they do not want there to be a God to believe in. But this refusal to let God be God and exercise his right to be the loving ruler of our lives can have its religious forms as well. This is not so much an outright denial that God exists, but a remaking of the idea of god so he becomes domesticated; the god we would like there to be, one who would indulge us without making demands upon us. The result is the same: our owner is cut out of our world because we want to manage our own 'vineyard' without any divine interference. What is more, just let him try to meddle in our affairs and it will be all the worse for him! That, in effect, is the issue that Jesus is addressing in this parable.

GET THE PICTURE

This parable is not like the earlier parables of the kingdom such as that of the Sower. Those were more obscure riddles which needed a good deal of teasing out by the listeners. This parable is more of an allegory; it is a much clearer story where each item in the parable has a spiritual counterpart, a little like C. S. Lewis' *Chronicles of Narnia*. The earlier parables of Jesus had points which were more or less 'hidden', these later ones are more or less 'open'. Why? Because Jesus is drawing to the end of his ministry. As time has gone by he has steadily been unfolding to his followers both his identity and his mission. The turning point was in chapter 16 and Peter's great confession that Jesus is 'the Christ, the Son of the living God'. Jesus then goes on to explain that his purpose in coming into the world is to die as a sacrifice for sins and to rise again from the dead. Now he is in Jerusalem and opposition to him is mounting, as we see in verse 23. In response to Jesus having just hurled the money changers out from the temple, the religious establishment turn on him, demanding, 'By what authority do you do these things?' This allegory is, in part, a response to that challenge. This is why he has 'authority'—he is the Son and heir, and this is what his own people will do—kill him. Those listening picked up the message loud and clear as we can see in verse 45: 'When the chief priests and the Pharisees heard Jesus' parables, they knew he was talking about them'. Then what did they do? Feel guilty and change their ways? Not at all. They decided to do the very thing the parable warned they would do: 'They looked for a way to arrest him' (v. 46). Tragically, we have been doing the same ever since. The person and teaching of Jesus have proved so uncomfortable and so demanding that we feel that somehow he must be silenced. Silence him by changing his teaching—cutting out bits from the Bible. Silence him by reducing him to one of a group of religious leaders from which we can take our pick. Silence him by, in effect, killing him again, destroying his reputation, mocking his morality, saying he was a man for his day but not ours; we have moved on. As we shall see, these attempts at evasion are not only futile but dangerous.

A MESSAGE ABOUT THE PAST

The first thing we notice in this parable is that we have a message about the past:

> There was a landowner who planted a vineyard. He put a wall around it, dug a winepress in it and built a watchtower. Then he rented the vineyard to some farmers and went away on a journey. When the harvest time approached, he sent his servants to the tenants to collect his fruit. The tenants seized his servants; they beat one, killed another, and stoned a third. Then he sent other servants to them, more than the first time, and the tenants treated them the same way. Last of all, he sent his son to them. 'They will respect my son,' he said.
>
> vv. 33–7

Vines and vineyards were a familiar part of everyday Palestinian life. Here we have an account of one with an absentee landlord, which has been given over to tenants who were meant to hand over some of the produce as part of their annual rent. But they have other plans. They want most, if not all, of the profits themselves and they are not subtle in making the point. When the rent collector arrives they beat him up. And this goes on and on until eventually the son of the owner comes along and they seize this as an opportunity to take control of the ownership of the vineyard altogether. They take a calculated risk in murdering him, gambling on the owner being weak-willed, elderly or too far away to take decisive action. After all, in Jewish law a person who could prove three year's undisputed possession of a property could claim ownership of it, and these tenants banked on that happening. It is a miserable and vile story. The behaviour of these men makes the Mafia look like the Vienna Boy's Choir in comparison!

In fact, it is far worse than that, because the property of which Jesus speaks is God's property and those who have constantly tried to cheat him of it are God's people. It had been going on for at least 800 years. In Isaiah 5: 1–2 we read, 'My loved one had a vineyard on a fertile hillside. He dug it up and cleared it of stones and planted it with the choicest vines. He built a watchtower in it and cut out a winepress as well. Then he looked for a crop of good grapes, but it yielded only bad fruit.' The wording is more or less identical to verse 33. Who is Isaiah talking about, and thus who is Jesus discussing? He goes on to tell us: 'The vineyard of the LORD Almighty is the house of Israel, and the men of Judah are the garden of his delight.' Do you see how scandalous this is? This is Israel, God's own people who were meant to be his pride and joy. They should have been producing spiritual fruit, which should have made all the other nations sit up and take notice, so they would seek God and find him. But that did not happen. They decided to rewrite the laws. Many of the leaders kept up with religious rigmarole but lied and cheated their way through life, taking bribes and robbing people of justice, especially the weak and vulnerable. And when God did send prophets— his rent collectors—to plead with them and warn them to change their ways, they beat them up. Isaiah, so tradition has it, was sawn in two, Jeremiah was imprisoned in a pit, and on the rebellion went with other prophets.

The tragedy is that it was the same in Jesus' day. John the Baptist was beheaded and the greatest of them all, the Son, was utterly abhorred.

But this is not simply a description of Israel. It is also a description of our world and our nation, and it may well also be a description of our lives. The book of Genesis tells us that when God created man and woman, he placed them in a garden that he had specially prepared for them. He gave them the privilege of being his co-workers to take care of the garden and to enjoy all its benefits. But that was not enough for them, they wanted to be the sole owners, they wanted to be like God, not so much being lawbreakers but lawmakers; they wanted to decide what they wanted to do. The result was what is known as the 'fall', the downward spiritual and moral spiral which we see in evidence all around us today. What does living without God look like? It looks like Bosnia, Afghanistan, Zimbabwe, the Congo.

In the past, God has singularly blessed Great Britain as a nation. For a thousand years, Christianity has been the official faith of this land. We have been delivered from paganism in the distant past, from Islam in the Middle Ages, from a corrupt Roman Catholicism in the sixteenth century and from Fascist and Marxist dictatorships in the twentieth century. Christianity gave us our schools, our hospitals, our prison reforms and factory acts. Blessing upon blessing has come our way. But what have we done with them? Thanked the Giver? Hardly. We have taken them for granted, spurned his love, privatised religion, and so our society steadily unravels with new laws now having to be introduced to control eight-year-olds. How far we have fallen.

But you may wish to ask yourself: 'How kind has God been in my life?' Yet, still there are areas you will not let God into, there are secret sins you are busy nursing. The owner of your life might be allowed to have some fruit, but not all that is his by right. Is that what is happening?

If so, then look again at this story. Do you see how much God is showing his patience with his people—how much he loves them? He sends messenger after messenger, and in one last act, we read in verse 37, he sent his son to them (in the original it reads 'the son'—his one and only son), saying, 'They will respect my son.' That is how much God cares for a wayward world and wayward people—he is willing to send his only son. Could we want any greater evidence of God's love and care for us than that? Perhaps. So let us look at what happens to this son in verses 38–9.

A MESSAGE FOR THE PRESENT

> But when the tenants saw the son, they said to each other, 'This is the heir. Come, let's kill him and take his inheritance'. So they took him and threw him out of the vineyard and killed him.

What convinces me of the untold potential for humans to do evil—what theologians call 'original sin'? Is it the murders by Fred West? Is it what we would see if you were to go to Auschwitz today, the thousands of pounds of women's hair, the gas ovens, the pictures of abused children, and clothing stacked to the ceiling? In part, yes. But what convinces me most of the wickedness which resides in the human heart is that when it came down to it, we murdered our Maker. That is what the cross, the killing of the Son outside the vineyard means. It is the ultimate insult, the supreme gesture of human contempt for the rule of God. It is the final snub which puts the lid on all the snubs that God has received from the human race.

At this point it would be all too easy to shelter behind the fact that Jesus' message was for his own present time—addressing first century Jews. 'Oh yes', we say, 'it was all their fault. The Jews, the Romans, we all know how barbaric they were.'

Do you remember that old Negro spiritual? 'Were you there when they crucified my Lord?' Spiritually, we were there. Some of us were with the Roman bureaucrats—turning a blind eye to the injustice, as some of us turn a blind eye to the evidence for Jesus today. Some of us were amongst the smug religious leaders, impeccable in our orthodoxy, but wanting rid of a disturbing Messiah for the sake of a quiet life. But I guess most of us were with the crowd, maybe the same crowd that only a few days earlier had been shouting 'Hosanna' when all seemed to be going well, but who were now shouting 'Crucify, crucify'. Our hands were not the actual hands that drove the nails into his hands and feet, but it was our sin that held him there nonetheless. In his mercy he cried out, 'Father, forgive them, for they do not know what they are doing' (Luke 23: 34). But this parable shows us the remarkable grace of that prayer, for they did know what they were doing, as we see in verse 35. If there was any ignorance, it was a culpable ignorance. We living today have even less excuse than they had for we have the whole Bible in our hands, God's complete and clear revelation. We also have had two thousand years of the good that Christianity has done. So for us to walk away from Christ, is to add our own nail to the cross.

A MESSAGE REGARDING THE FUTURE

This is why Jesus gives a message regarding the future: '"Therefore, when the owner of the vineyard comes, what will he do to those tenants?" "He will bring those wretches to a wretched end," they replied, "and he will rent the vineyard to other tenants, who will give him his share of the crop at harvest time."' (vv. 40–4). Who answered Jesus' question about the action of the landowner? It was the chief priests and the Pharisees. They had brought condemnation upon themselves. Jesus did not give the answer—they did, and so they are without excuse. They can spot a criminal act when they see one, but the tragedy is they cannot see it applies to themselves. Therefore, Jesus spells it out for them with three references from Old Testament scriptures, which Jesus takes as God's own authority in verse 42. First, a quotation from Psalm 118: 'The stone the builders rejected has become a capstone; the Lord has done this, and it is marvellous in our eyes' (Psalm 118: 22-3). In other words, on the building site the builders throw to one side a stone which they think is useless. Then they realise that this is the cornerstone, the one stone which holds everything else in place. This 'stone' is what God uses to build his new spiritual house—the new Israel, the church. Here Jesus may be engaging in wordplay, because in Aramaic, the language Jesus spoke, the word for 'son' is 'ben' and the word for stone is 'eben'—so the 'ben' which is thrown out and killed, is the 'eben' which God raises up to build a house. Here there is a hint that the death of the Son is not the end, but that the scriptures, including Psalm 118, point to a resurrection. Therefore, those who trust the Son receive the blessings of the son: 'Therefore I tell you that the kingdom of God will be taken away from you and given to a people [or nation] who will produce its fruit' (v. 43). Who are these people? Well, not the present Jewish religious establishment. As they have rejected the Son, so God will reject them. But their future is worse than that, hence the next quotation which is a combination of a passage from the prophet Daniel (2: 44 ff.) and Isaiah (8: 14): 'He who falls on this stone will be broken to pieces, but he on whom it falls will be crushed'. In other words, for those who accept Jesus he becomes a cornerstone which restores them, but for those who reject him that same stone becomes a rock which will crush them. It is the same person, Jesus, but he occupies two different roles depending upon our response to him: he is either our saviour or our judge. The judgement he makes is simply the judgement that we know is right: 'He will bring those wretches to a wretched end' (v. 41).

How do you stand in relation to Jesus, God's Son? Do you welcome him as the rightful ruler of your life and the world? Do you believe God wants the best for you? Are you offering up the fruit of your lives to him, saying,

'Lord I want to do this for your glory'? Or like Aldous Huxley and these good religious folk in the story, are you keeping God at a distance, denying him access? Because one day he is going to demand access, and then it will be too late. There is no life better than the Christian life, there is no love greater than God's love and there is no greater privilege than being God's tenants.

12

An Offer Not to be Refused

Matthew 22

A national newspaper told the story of a couple who had planned a holiday of a lifetime, but who found themselves having a completely different holiday because of a major mistake. Emma Nunn and her boyfriend, Raoul Sebastian, had been saving for months for a special trip to Sydney, Australia. They would see the Sydney Opera House, the beautiful Bondai beach and many of the other attractions Australia had to offer. When they set off on their trip, however, they found something was terribly wrong. Instead of flying round the world to Sydney, they ended up flying to Canada. At that point they were not too bothered since they had got their tickets cheaply and they thought that this was just a longer way to Australia. When they got to Canada, they were told to get on a tiny propeller powered plane which would take them to their final destination. It was then that they began to panic: 'Surely this propeller-powered plane is not going to take us all the way to Australia from Canada?' they thought. Sure enough, when they got to their destination, they found they were not in Sydney, Australia, but Sydney, Nova Scotia, a small mining town in northern Canada, with next to nothing for tourists. The mix-up had happened at the ticket agency which sent them to the right destination, Sydney, but the wrong country: Canada instead of Australia! One mistake had huge consequences.

Jesus tells a parable in Matthew 22 which makes the same point: wrong decisions can have huge consequences, only this time we see the consequences are eternal. He begins his story in verse 2 with the familiar phrase: 'The kingdom of heaven is like...' Jesus is telling another parable about the saving reign of God; a parable about what it means to come under the kingly rule of God. This parable of the wedding banquet is about a mistake that the leaders of God's people were making; a mistake of eternal proportions. Since Matthew 21: 23, Jesus has been talking to the chief priests and the elders. These were the religious leaders of the day, the clergy and bishops of Israel. He has told them two parables about a vineyard in chapter 21. Firstly, there was a parable about a vineyard owner and his two sons, and secondly a parable about a vineyard owner and his tenants. Both have been aimed at the religious establishment that Jesus is talking to. His conclusion comes in 21: 43, and it is very stark: 'the kingdom of God will be taken away from you and given to a people who will produce its fruit.' What he is saying is that the kingdom of God will be taken from these religious leaders and given to others.

That is shocking. These people thought they were going to be part of God's universal reign, and yet Jesus turns round and says to them: 'You are going to be excluded.' It would be like Jesus getting up at a meeting of the house of bishops with all the bishops in England gathered round him and saying: 'You think you lot are going to heaven, don't you? Actually, the reality is you are going to hell. And your places in heaven which you thought you'd reserved by your impressive deeds and religious credentials are going to be given to others.' That would be shocking. But that is what Jesus is saying to these religious officials.

Why is Jesus saying these things? What have these religious leaders done to make them subject to Jesus' criticism? Jesus tells another parable to explain exactly what they have done. Their problem is they have made two terrible mistakes which will have huge implications. This is far more serious than getting on the wrong plane and ending up in Canada. It is a matter of being on the wrong road and ending up in hell. We shall find that it is just as possible for men and women like us in the twenty-first century to make the same mistakes. So this parable of Jesus is not in Matthew's gospel for mere historical interest. It is here to warn us not to make the same mistakes as the religious leaders of Jesus' day.

THE INVITATION IS REJECTED

The first mistake made is that the invitation is rejected in verses 1–10. Jesus' story is about a king who wanted to give a wedding banquet for his son who was getting married. In those days, the groom's father picked up the tab and sent out the invitations, and so it is here. It seems some invitations have been sent out already. What happens in verse 3 is that those who had been invited are now told to come. It is a bit like inviting friends to a party at your house for the next weekend, and saying, 'I'll be in touch nearer the time with the final details.' So, sure enough, on Saturday afternoon, you ring up your friends to tell them to come because everything is ready. In the same way, the King sends out his servants to tell everyone that the banquet is ready. The wine is uncorked, the orchestra is tuning up, the fireworks are lined up and the beef roast is slowly turning. Everything is ready. What happens? Verse 3: 'But they refused to come.' Maybe there has been some misunderstanding. So verse 4: 'Then he sent some more servants and said, "Tell those who have been invited that I have prepared my dinner: My oxen and fattened cattle have been butchered, and everything is ready. Come to the wedding banquet."' This time the king lets them know what is on the menu: roast beef, the finest veal steak money can buy, washed down with a fruity wine. Surely they will come now? But no: 'But they paid no attention and went off—one to his field, another to his business. The rest seized his servants, mistreated them and killed them' (vv. 5–6). Can you believe it? What a terrible way to respond to an invitation to a party. Not surprisingly, the king is furious: 'The king was enraged. He sent his army and destroyed those murderers and burned their city' (v. 7). Of course, the king cannot let all that lovely food go to waste, so he tells his servants to go round the streets and invite anyone they find. And that is what happens: 'So the servants went out into the streets and gathered all the people they could find, both good and bad, and the wedding hall was filled with guests' (v. 10). The original guests have rejected the invitation, and the king gets others to come to the feast.

Why, then, did Jesus tell this parable? As we have already seen, the parable is about the kingdom of God. God is the king and Jesus his son, and he is talking about entry into his eternal reign; how to get into God's kingdom. The first mistake the religious leaders made is that they rejected the invitation. According to Jesus, there are two consequences of that rejection.

GOD'S GRACE IS SPURNED

The first consequence is that God's undeserved love is spurned. The king in this story did not just send out his servants once. He did not say 'one chance was enough'. He sent them out a second time. He gave the guests plenty of opportunity to respond. That is exactly what God did for Israel. Time and again, God sent his prophets in the Old Testament to tell the people that one day God's rescuer would come and they would all be able to come to the feast in heaven at the end of time. God gave his people plenty of opportunity to get ready for the day when the feast was ready. He is a God of great grace and generosity. When Jesus arrived, that time had come. He was the one who could bring the people to the feast. Through his death on the cross there could be forgiveness of sins and entry into heaven. So they should trust in Jesus and come to the feast. But the people of Israel, led by their religious leaders, rejected him. They refused to come to the feast.

Some rejected God's grace out of cold apathy. Like some guests in the story, they said they had better things to do: their businesses and personal problems were far more important than accepting Jesus and coming to the feast. Others were openly hostile to Jesus. Either side of this parable, in 21: 45–6 and 22: 15, we are told the leaders were trying to kill Jesus. Eventually they would succeed. They spurned the grace of God shown to them in Jesus. Jesus was the only way that they could get to the feast; the only way that they could come into God's eternal reign, and they rejected the invitation.

Those same characteristics are seen today in people's response to Jesus. Some reject him out of cold apathy; they just cannot be bothered to give Jesus a second glance. Their own lives are too important for them to bother. Others are openly hostile to the grace of God shown in Jesus. Whichever the reaction is, it is spurning God's grace. The God who lovingly seeks to rescue sinful people like you and me is shoved out of the way.

Just imagine for one moment that a new sports hall and health centre was built in your town. You discover the Queen is going to open it. It is a brand-new complex with gym, swimming pool, saunas and full-time masseurs. As the Queen steps out of her car, all the dignitaries and people line up. But then, as she walks up that line, an extraordinary thing happens: one by one the people spit in the Queen's face. Can you imagine the outrage?

If we would never snub the Queen in that way, then why do we snub the King of kings in that way? If you are a Christian playing with sin and not being ruthless with it in your life, then you are snubbing God in that way; saying that his rule in your life does not matter. Maybe cold apathy is creeping into your Christian life: Bible reading is taking a back seat; church is becoming a chore. Realise what you are doing. Do not snub the King of kings. Do not spurn his grace to you in these ways. If you are not a Christian and you are continuing to turn your back on God's offer to you, then you, too, are snubbing God in the most offensive way possible. Maybe you are saying, 'Life's too busy to go for this Christianity business too keenly.' Or perhaps you are thinking: 'It's not relevant to me. It's OK for the religious type people, but not for me.' If you are not bothered to give God a look-in, or if you are more concerned with running your life your way, then you are spitting in God's face and saying, 'I don't want anything to do with your invitation to the feast.' You are spurning the grace of God. You are tearing up the invitation and shoving it back in God's face. Whether it is cold apathy or open hostility, it is all the same to God. You are spurning his grace.

GOD'S JUDGEMENT IS SEEN

There is a terrible consequence of doing that, because the second result of rejecting the invitation is seeing God's judgement. In the story, the king sends his servants and they kill the people who rejected the invitation. The prophets of the Old Testament used this sort of language to warn of God's judgement at the end of time. The religious leaders would face God's judgement for rejecting the invitation. It stands as a serious warning to us, that if we reject God's offer, then we, too, will face his judgement.

This is not just a question of personal taste. We cannot say that God may be important to some but not to me. Because, like it or not, the God of the Bible is the true and living God before whom we will all one day stand. Amazingly, however, this God offers us a place at his eternal feast today. The king's son wants to see you there. The banquet will be full of people. The question is, will we accept the invitation? The party will go on with or without us. So, whatever we do, we are not to make the same mistake as the religious leaders. They rejected the invitation and, in doing so, they spurned God's grace and they saw God's judgement. If we reject the invitation, whether by cold apathy or open hostility, we, too, will spurn God's grace and face his judgement.

THE DRESS CODE IS IGNORED

The parable, however, does not stop there. We could be forgiven for thinking that was the end of the story. Either we accept the invitation or reject it. That is it. But Jesus goes on in verses 11–13 to highlight another mistake that the religious leaders are making and one which we also make: the dress code is ignored. Sometimes when you get invited to a party there are two instructions on the invitation. One says RSVP, you must respond, and Jesus has tackled that instruction in the first half of the parable. Yet there is often a dress code on the invitation as well. It may be a seventies party, so you have to dress accordingly, or it may be fancy dress, so you need to dress properly. If you turn up to the party in the wrong clothes, then you are going to look a fool. There is a dress code to be followed. Jesus is saying in the second half of this parable that there is a particular dress code for heaven. We must take care to note what it is, otherwise we will not get in to the party.

With the wedding banquet in heaven there is something striking about what happens to those who are not wearing the right clothes:

> But when the king came in to see the guests, he noticed a man there who was not wearing wedding clothes. 'Friend', he asked, 'how did you get in here without wedding clothes?' The man was speechless. Then the king told the attendants, 'Tie him hand and foot, and throw him outside, into the darkness, where there will be weeping and gnashing of teeth.'
>
> vv. 11–13

At God's wedding feast, if we are not wearing the right clothes, Jesus says we will find ourselves going to hell. That is what the language means in verse 13, when it mentions weeping and gnashing of teeth. We have seen it before in Matthew 13. It is only used by Jesus, and he is talking about hell; the place for those who reject God's kind offer of forgiveness and heaven.

But we may say, 'Come on, Jesus, it's a bit harsh isn't it? Maybe this man simply misread the invitation. Maybe he didn't have time to change, having just come in from the street corners. Go easy on him!' But flouting the dress code is clearly serious. Why?

The Bible teaches us that all our righteous acts, all our good deeds, are like filthy rags. We are not fit to go to God's wedding feast because we are not dressed properly. Our lives are messed up by sin and disobedience to God. But the amazing thing is that God is willing to give us new clothes. He is willing to dress us in perfection. He is willing to give us forgiveness. We can be holy, we can be like God. We can go to his feast, because through Jesus' death on the cross we can be washed clean and dressed properly. But this man in our story arrogantly rejected the king's offer of new clothes and waltzed into the feast wearing his own clothes. That was precisely what the religious leaders of Jesus day were doing. They, too, were arrogantly assuming that they could come to the feast on their own terms. They thought they were good enough for God. They thought they were nice enough and religious enough for God. But Jesus tells them sternly: 'Unless you are humble enough to accept the King's clothes, unless you are humble enough to come to Jesus and receive the forgiveness he offers and the new life he promises, you will be thrown out of God's presence for ever.' That is the price of rejecting the invitation and ignoring the dress code.

Sadly, many twenty-first century men and women make this mistake too. It is possible for the non-Christian and the professing Christian to be in danger of ignoring the dress code of heaven. For the non-Christian, one might guess that most people would say they want to accept the invitation and go to heaven, but are unwilling to submit to God's dress code and humbly admit their complete inability to get themselves to heaven. Many people still believe that they are good enough for God. They are 'decent people' and God is 'nice enough to let them into heaven.' They have never broken any of the commandments in a serious way, and they are kind and upstanding members of the community. If that is what you think, then look again at what Jesus teaches: unless you accept the invitation on God's terms, unless you accept his offer of fresh clothes, forgiveness and a fresh start though him, then you will not be at the party in heaven; you will find yourself in hell. It is a huge offence to the king to ignore the dress code, to ignore the clothes of forgiveness and holiness that he graciously gives you. Surely that is too good an offer to refuse. Wonderfully, God's invitation goes out to many, but few accept the invitation and take note of the dress code. Many are invited but few are chosen. Make sure you are not one those.

Charles Spurgeon was one of those who accepted the invitation and respected the dress code of heaven. Spurgeon lived in the nineteenth century and, as a young man, was brought up to believe in Christian truth. He classed himself as a good person and one who knew all about Christianity. Yet, for many years, he had been afflicted with a terrible feeling of not being good enough for God. He was acutely aware of his own failings and his inability to live up to God's perfect standards. He once said of himself: 'I thought I would rather have been a frog or a toad than have been made a man. I reckoned that the most defiled creature was a better thing than myself, for I had sinned against Almighty God.' One day he came to hear of the forgiveness that is offered to us through Jesus' death on the cross. Spurgeon happened to be in a church in Colchester one Christmas. The regular preacher had got stuck in the snow. So one man got up who was no preacher. In fact, Spurgeon in his autobiography says he was downright stupid. His sermon simply consisted in repeating over and again in slightly different ways the verse of the Bible that he was preaching on: 'Look unto me, and you will be saved.' But as the preacher was running out of things to say after ten minutes, he looked directly at Spurgeon and said: 'Young man you look very miserable and you will always be miserable unless you look to Jesus. You have nothing to do but to look to Jesus.' That was what Spurgeon did that day. He realised it was only in Jesus that his sins could be taken away. Only by accepting Jesus' offer of forgiveness and receiving his new clothes could he be freed from sin and given new life. That is what happened. Spurgeon was a changed man from that day. He accepted the invitation on God's terms and obeyed the dress code.

There is a warning here also for the person who claims to be a Christian to not ignore the dress code. There is a danger for those of us who profess to be Christians to come to God on our own terms. It is a 'yes, but...' sort of faith. It is a faith which says: 'Yes, I'll accept your forgiveness Lord, but I don't want you to have all my life. Yes, I'll accept the invitation Lord, but I don't want to give you too much of my time. Once a week's enough isn't it? I've done my bit. Yes, I'll accept the invitation Lord, but I want control of my relationships and I'll decide when it's time to tell everyone at work I'm a Christian. Yes, Lord, I'll accept the invitation, but I don't want it to be too uncomfortable. I think I'll retain control of just how keen I become.' The problem with the 'yes, but...' type of faith is that you are in danger of ignoring the dress code of heaven. You are in danger of treating your faith like just another hobby: some play golf; some are Christians. But when the King of kings calls you to his wedding feast, you must accept on his terms. Otherwise, you will find yourself leaving by the back door. Do not make the same mistake as the religious leaders. Do not ignore the dress code.

Ultimately, if we get on the wrong plane, it is just a minor inconvenience. But Jesus tells this parable to warn us not to make mistakes of catastrophic proportions. It is not our holiday that is at stake, but our eternal destinies.

13

Be Ready

Matthew 25: 31–46

The Turner prize for art is normally a focus for controversy and 2001 was no exception. The £20,000 prize went to Martin Creed who, according to the *Guardian*, is 'famous for his composition in using everyday materials. He is keen to recapture the original spirit of conceptual art (where it is the thought that counts) and has shown plenty of works that are no more than sheets of paper with a few words on.' His portfolio for the prize included a screwed-up newspaper, a piece of blue tack impressed with a thumbprint, and his centrepiece winning work, entitled 'Lights going on and off', described exactly what it was: lights going on and off! This has led many to wonder what criteria the judges use to determine what constitutes 'good art'.

A few years ago the competence of some other judges was brought into question when an unknown artist was showcased by the Manchester Academy of Fine Arts. The judges then selected a watercolour entitled, 'Rhythm of the Trees', which displayed, they opined, a certain quality of colour balance, composition, and technical skill. The artist, as it turned out, was a four-year-old child.

When it comes to the matter of being assessed, whether it is our car for an MOT, our child's education for their GCSEs, or our state of health carried out by an MD, we have a right to expect the best; people who know what they are doing and who will do it well without fear or favour. How much more, then, should we expect only the best when it comes to our lives being assessed at the end of time, when what is at stake is not simply our future reputation but our eternal destiny?

In Matthew 25: 31 ff. we discover exactly what will happen. Judgement day is coming. The vital question it raises is: will we be ready? This raises a further question: how can we be ready? That, in part, is the question this penetrating picture painted by Jesus answers.

Is this a 'proper' parable? Scholars debate the issue. Some view it is a discourse with 'parabolic features', others as a parable with similarities to other parables of Jesus. This shows how difficult it can be to devise a neat definition of a parable. Given the content matter about judgement day and the final 'unveiling' of the King, perhaps we can call it an 'apocalyptic parable'. Whatever, that Jesus teaches here in story form in no way diminishes the awesome reality depicted, rather, the imagery intensifies the nature of what Jesus refers to. If the figurative nature of the language is profoundly disturbing in places, will not the reality be more disturbing still? We are to allow the imagery to make us think deeply about where we stand on this great divide.

THE JUDGE

Note some of the terms Jesus uses to describe himself on that dreadful day: 'When the *Son of Man* comes in his glory, and all the angels with him, he will sit on his throne in heavenly glory' (v. 31). 'Then the *King* will say to those on his right, "Come, you who are blessed by *my Father*"' (v. 34).

Artists should judge artists. Car mechanics should assess cars. And teachers assess their pupils. Who, then, should judge human beings? Ideally, the answer would be a fellow human being, someone who has walked this weary war-torn world of ours and has known the pull of temptation, the disappointment of love betrayed, and the grief of loved ones lost. What is needed is someone who has experienced the whole gamut of human emotions, its troughs and its peaks, who has wrestled with all the struggles common to humanity and triumphed. Only then would they be in a position to say, 'I understand exactly your situation; I have been there too.' That is precisely what the world is presented with in Jesus Christ who took to himself the title 'Son of Man', a phrase which in part captures the idea that he is one of us. But it is a term which goes beyond a mere identification of the species 'Homo sapiens', for it also denotes someone who represents us. This is humanity's federal head. As Adam once represented mankind in a Garden, Jesus now represents us in heaven. The primary background for this figure is Daniel 7:

> In my vision at night I looked, and there before me was one like a son of man, coming with the clouds of heaven. He approached the Ancient of Days and was led into his presence. He was given authority, glory and sovereign power; all peoples, nations and men of every language worshipped him. His dominion is an everlasting dominion that will not pass away, and his kingdom is one that will never be destroyed.
>
> Dan. 7: 13–14

This is a comforting thought. We are never too impressed with someone who comes along trying to tell us what we should or should not do without having proved themselves on the ground. Rather caustically, George Bernard Shaw put it this way: 'Those who can, do. Those who can't, teach. Those who can't teach, teach teachers.' It may be a little cynical but there is more than a grain of truth in that saying. Yet no such thing can be said of this judge. He has been through it all. Born into the filth of a cattle shed, stumbling as he takes his first steps, dribbling as he is fed, only to be impaled on a stake when he is fully grown, forsaken by his friends, left naked and bleeding for all the world to see as he dies. This is the 'Suffering Son of man' of Isaiah 53: 2–3:

> He grew up before him like a tender shoot, and like a root out of dry ground. He had no beauty or majesty to attract us to him, nothing in his appearance that we should desire him. He was despised and rejected by men, a man of sorrows, and familiar with suffering. Like one from whom men hide their faces he was despised, and we esteemed him not.

A human judge, however, no matter how virtuous, is not sufficient as humankind's judge. Not only is experiential knowledge required whereby the person can fully identify with us, but also divine knowledge so that he can fully assess us. This we have in Jesus. In Matthew 25: 34 he speaks of 'My Father'. This is not only the Son of Man, this is also the unique Son of God. His knowledge is infallible, his judgements impeccable, and his wisdom inscrutable. He knows everything about us. If we have mitigating circumstances, he is aware of them. In the glory of his omniscience he has followed our progress from the moment we were conceived: 'My frame was not hidden from you when I was made in the secret place. When I was woven together in the depths of the earth, your eyes saw my unformed body' (Ps. 139: 15). As man, he knows experientially from the inside what it is like to be human; as God, he knows infallibly from the outside what it is like to be me. Can you think of anyone better qualified to judge you than a person like that? Here is someone who, in one person, combines fully the divine and human natures—all-knowing, all-wise, all-just. That is the Lord Jesus Christ.

Not only is Jesus qualified to judge, he has every right to judge. He is 'the King'. Adam was meant to be the one who was to rule this world with love and fairness (Gen. 1)—he failed, but Jesus succeeds. God has made him the rightful ruler of this planet and all its inhabitants. As Peter puts it in his Pentecost sermon: 'Therefore let all Israel be assured of this: God has made this Jesus, whom you crucified, both Lord and Christ' (Acts 2: 36). Our lives are therefore not our own with which to do whatever we please, they belong to Another. He owns us and so has the right to judge us.

THE JUDGED

What is the make-up of those who will be judged? We are told in verse 32: 'All the nations will be gathered before him, and he will separate the people from one another as a shepherd separates the sheep from the goats. He will put the sheep on his right side and the goats on his left.' Here we have a mix of powerful and evocative imagery.

Firstly, there is the image of the all-conquering King who gathers his new subjects around him to determine those who have been loyal to him and who will therefore continue in his kingdom. There are also those who are designated traitors and who are therefore to be banished.

The second picture is of a shepherd. During the day, he allows goats to come in, to mingle and graze with his flock of sheep, but at night, when they are to settle down in their folds, he separates them out, allowing only the sheep to go in. This is not as easy as it sounds because Palestinian goats look much like Palestinian sheep.

So the question both images present us with is this: How is the Shepherd-King to decide who the loyal subjects are and who are the rebels? How can he tell the sheep from the goats? They both smell dire and bleat. What is the basis for deciding to which of these two groups people belong? It is important to notice that there are only two groups: those placed on the right of the King and those placed on his left; the right hand of a Near-Eastern monarch signifying approval and the left hand denoting condemnation.

We are forced to ask, who are the righteous in verse 37? Who are the cursed destined for eternal darkness in verse 41? Is what qualifies us for the former group simply a matter of being religious? Is it a question of calling yourself a Christian and paying lip-service to orthodoxy? Not according to Jesus. Here he turns our expectations upside down.

THE JUDGEMENT

At first sight it might appear that Jesus merely confirms our expectations (v. 34):

> Then the King will say to those on his right, 'Come, you who are blessed by my Father; take your inheritance, the kingdom prepared for you since the creation of the world. For I was hungry and you gave me something to eat, I was thirsty and you gave me something to drink, I was a stranger and you invited me in, I needed clothes and you clothed me, I was sick and you looked after me, I was in prison and you came to visit me.'

And then again in verse 41:

> Then he will say to those on his left, 'Depart from me, you who are cursed, into the eternal fire prepared for the devil and his angels. For I was hungry and you gave me nothing to eat, I was thirsty and you gave me nothing to drink, I was a stranger and you did not invite me in, I needed clothes and you did not clothe me, I was sick and in prison and you did not look after me.'

Is it not widely held that for those who do believe in a heaven of sorts, it is populated by good people, such as those who care for the sick and needy and who visit those in prison and hospital? By contrast, it is the mean and selfish that do not do any of these things who will have their come-uppance on judgement day. Consequently, heaven is full of nice people and hell is full of bad people. It therefore looks like you can be just as good a Christian not going to church, so long as you are kind to one another. Is that what Jesus is saying? It is how some would read this passage. They speak of the 'anonymous Christian'. This is the idea that on the day of judgement Christ will accept the good Buddhist who has never even heard of him because of his good deeds.

He may not have realised it, but simply by being generous to the poor he was being generous to Jesus, and so the doors of heaven are thrown open wide to such as him.

If that is so, then we have a major problem because that idea flatly contradicts everything else the New Testament teaches, namely, that we are saved by grace. Salvation is not merited at all, it is a gift received solely through putting our faith in Christ's work on the cross. We contribute nothing to our salvation except our sin, which necessitates it.

This, however, needs to be qualified.

The first qualification is that the Bible does make a link between faith and works; what we claim to believe and what we actually do. So while we are not saved by good works, we are saved for good works (Eph. 2: 10). It is bordering on the blasphemous to say, 'Yes, I believe in Jesus. Yes, I believe he died for my sins, but I will not allow it to make any difference to the way I behave at work, or treat my wife, or fill in my tax return.' Yet, sadly, that is precisely what some professing Christians do. The final judgement will expose such hypocrisy.

The second qualification demands that we pay close attention to what the passage says by noting the detail. We then discover the simple equation, good works equals heavenly reward, is too simple by far.

Jesus speaks these words to his disciples who want to know about the lead-up to the end of the world. They, like most of his audience at the time, were Jews. As far as they were concerned, it was a matter of belonging to the right group, which meant belonging to Israel, even becoming an honorary Jew through circumcision and keeping the ritual, that made you one of God's sheep. But Jesus here speaks of 'all the nations', literally, all the 'pagans', and from some of these comes God's sheep, members of the kingdom. Therefore, membership of this kingdom is no longer based upon national affiliation or religious heritage. What is more, this inheritance spoken of in verse 34, in which the righteous are to share—the happiness of God—has been prepared for them since before the world was made, before they were even born. This seems to hint at the gracious nature of the 'reward'.

What are the reasons given for God accepting some but not others? How do we know whether we are a sheep or a goat? The answer is found in verses 35 and 45, and it is all to do with people's true attitude towards the King as revealed by their actions towards his subjects.

The King says to his people in verse 35, 'For, ['here is the basis for my judgement'] I was hungry and you gave me something to eat, I was thirsty and you gave me something to drink, I was a stranger and you invited me in' and so on. They are doing things to Jesus, the King. How? 'When did this take place?' they ask. They do not recall seeing the King in their streets. Verse 40 gives the answer: 'Whatever you did for one of the least of these brothers of mine, you did it for me.' Who, then, are these brothers of the King? To answer that question we need to visit two other earlier sayings of Jesus. Matthew 12: 49 records the first: 'Whoever does the will of my Father in heaven is my brother and sister.' When Jesus speaks of 'the least of these' it is similar to what he says in chapter 10 when he is speaking of people accepting his disciples as his messengers, and so Jesus, the King himself: 'If anyone gives even a cup of cold water to one of these little ones because he is my disciple, I tell you the truth, he will certainly not lose his reward' (10: 42). Here, then, is the criterion Jesus will use as a basis for judgement: whether we accept and love the Lord Jesus. And whether we accept and love him is gauged not so much by what we say but by how much we love and care for fellow believers, especially those in need. This would include those who bring God's message to us, who are often the ones thrown into prison or struggling in poverty, as evidenced by the apostles themselves. As Jesus said elsewhere to his disciples, 'Whoever accepts anyone I send accepts me; and whoever accepts me accepts the one who sent me' (John 13: 20).

At Christmas 1534 Martin Luther spoke these words:

> There are many who think: 'If only I had been there. How quick I would have been to help the baby. I would have washed his linen. How happy I would have been to go with the shepherds to see the Lord lying in the manger'. Yes you would. You say that because you know how great Christ is, but if you had been there at the time you would have been no better than the people of Bethlehem. Childish and silly thoughts are these. Why don't you do it now? You have Christ in your neighbour.

When you are at church, there is Christ with you. You have Christ in the lonely Christian widow, the bewildered Christian teenager, the isolated Christian asylum seeker.

Notice how these people who are placed at Jesus' right hand and told to come in and enjoy the Father's blessing for all eternity are not conscious of doing these things. It is not as if they had thought to themselves, 'Oh I must ask that Christian into my home this Christmas because that is going to earn me a few points by inviting Jesus in.' No, they did what came naturally. This is the authentic mark of a Christian—they love one another and they show it.

But what of the others, the goats? What did they do? The irony is they did nothing. 'When did we see you hungry or thirsty or a stranger or needing clothes or sick or in prison?' (v. 44). And the King will reply, 'whatever you did not do for one of the least of these, you did not do for me' (v. 45). It is the 'least' of Jesus' brothers they overlooked, the ones they did not consider worth considering. They were invisible to them. You can be sure that amongst this crowd gathered before the Son of Man there will be those who would have numbered themselves as Christian—they too call him 'Lord' (v. 44). By their inaction, however, they have shown they never embraced the Christian message in their hearts because it never affected their lives. Some, no doubt, would be sound in orthodoxy, regular in church attendance, but showing no Christian charity where it counts most— to Christ's people in need. Is this an exaggeration? Can professing believers behave as Jesus describes here?

A few years ago, the wife of a London vicar wrote an article after they had moved to a parish, which had what was called a 'Bible-believing church'. She wrote:

> Eighteen months ago we were invited to a wedding where a large proportion of the 300 guests were clergy, not surprising, since bride and groom were Christian workers and the service was being conducted by a bishop. As we chattered, others asked how we were and how my husband had enjoyed his first six months. And almost without exception, the clergy and their spouses said to us, 'Oh, those first two years in a parish. How well we remember the hate-mail! The AGMs which ended in tears! The church wardens who tried to get rid of us.' Well, it's been two years now, and my husband has had enough interesting letters to paper his wall, including one complaining about a Christmas Day service before he got there; one moaning about our children's behaviour in church on a weekend they were away; one from a neighbour maintaining that we're such bad neighbours that it was the vicar's family, not the recession which reduced the value of the property, and one, our favourite, complaining about a guest service on the grounds that it was, most outrageously, full of guests.

It is good to report that under God the church has now been turned, but not without a price—the vicar's health. He now suffers from ME, which is not surprising. Here was a nice respectable church, full of nice respectable people, but who had no respect for Jesus, displayed by the fact that they had no respect for Jesus' servants.

There are only two destinations—eternal life and eternal punishment. Which destiny shall be ours depends upon our relationship with this King—Jesus. This is finally decided not by what we say, but by what we do. Changed lives, as well as professing lips, is what this King is looking for. He seeks radical Christianity, which is real Christianity, whereby we see the need of our Christian sister or brother and practically respond to it. This is the only measure Jesus will allow as the test of our love and devotion to him—the extent to which we love, and are devoted to, each other.